Parental Rights in Children's Medical Care

Where Is Our

FREEDOM

to Say No?

*A Look at the Injustice of the
American Medical System*

Shirley Cheng

Justice Found
An imprint of Dance with Your Heart! Publishing

*Dance with You
Heart! Publishing*

www.DanceWithYourHeart.com

Wappingers Falls, New York

ISBN: 978-0-6151-4994-3
Library of Congress Control Number: 2007904575

Justice Found
An imprint of Dance with Your Heart! Publishing

www.DanceWithYourHeart.com
Wappingers Falls, New York, United States of America

2

With my heart, I dedicate this book to an exceptionally brave and loving soul, my beloved mother Juliet Cheng, who has an invincible stamina to fight for my life till she holds victory in her hands. She is a fighter, a victor, but above all, she is a lover.

Table of Contents

Parental Rights in Children's Medical Care
Where Is Our Freedom to Say No?

What is a more frightening nightmare for parents than their children's illness? It is the fear of losing custody of their children.

In America, parents risk losing custody of their children forever when they disagree with doctors' recommended treatments or even when they want a second opinion.

Just ask the Wernecke family in Agua Dulce, Texas, whose daughter Katie was taken into state custody in 2005 when her parents refused radiation treatment for Katie's Hodgkin's disease. The same thing happened to Corissa Mueller in 2002, Tina Phifer in 1997, and a slew of other parents and children who have been victimized in the past decades.

My mother Juliet Cheng was one such parent whose child was forcefully and wrongly taken away by Child Protective Services over treatment disputes — not only once, but twice.

I was first taken from my mother when I was only twenty-two months old, when she insisted my doctor stop giving me aspirin (to treat juvenile rheumatoid arthritis), which only worsened my condition and caused severe side effects. The second incident occurred when I was seven years old, after she had wisely chosen not to follow a doctor's plan to operate on six of my joints in a single operation when the doctor did not even have any medication to effectively control my inflammation.

Fortunately, she won me back both times, so I was not forced to endure unnecessary and potentially harmful treatments that could have sent me to my grave.

The second custody case, in 1990, made international headlines. My mother and her lawyer, George Athanson—who had served as mayor of Hartford, Connecticut, for eleven years—appeared on the CBS *This Morning* show with Paula Zahn, and the story was reported on CNN, in the *New York Times*, *Newsweek*, the *Washington Post*, among many other major media outlets. She gained worldwide attention, including support from celebrities such as Katharine Hepburn and Taiwan's former first lady Soong May-ling.

When I was seven, I had no voice of my own. Now, seventeen years later, I am driven to speak for all the families who risk being torn apart for simply choosing to follow their own hearts and common sense in regards to their children's medical care. Everyone is a potential victim of this injustice when a child falls ill—including your own child or grandchild. I am here to help today's loving parents protect and keep custody of their children.

It is a crime when doctors force

unwanted or harmful treatments on children, and it is a violation against humanity when the state tears loving parents and children apart.

The American government needs to deal with each case according to its unique needs, instead of acting upon the same plan for all cases. Just because loving parents who disagree with medically recommended treatment does not mean that they are child abusers or that their child should be torn away from them. In this democratic land of independence, the child-protection laws in the medical system are extremely out of place.

America will be better if it gives freedom to devoted, competent parents. The average parent wants the best for their child. We, the patients in our own bodies and the caregivers who have cared for the patients for years, know what is best for us. Doctors may know what is the best treatment option for us, but even in all their certainty, they cannot force their knowledge and power on us.

So, what is the real issue here? Is it who loves the children the most (parents), or is it who believes they know what's medically best for the children (doctors)? I believe that question can only be answered by God. God created us, so He must know what is best for each and every one of us, but He gives us free will and the right to care for ourselves on our own. He lets every one of us decide for ourselves and choose what to do with our lives, even if it means that we make many mistakes.

He does not control us; He simply tells us how to be a good person and informs us of the consequences if we choose to be bad people.

But instead of allowing us the same free will that God gives us, our own people from the medical and legal systems take away our parental rights, snatching children away from parents — their primary source of love and care — in order to do what is "best" for the children. Worse yet, parents are not warned in advance what could happen if they dare disagree with a treatment plan. They are simply reported to Child Protective Services.

Can't we — parents and children — decide what is best for ourselves?

Where is our freedom to say no?

Firsthand Experiences

My mother experienced firsthand this injustice in the American medical system.

The first incident took place right before my first trip to China to seek emergent medical care, as the treatment I was receiving in America did nothing to lessen the intense pain I suffered from severe juvenile rheumatoid arthritis. The doctor I was seeing in America called Child Protective Services, claiming that my mother was abusing me. A CPS agent arrived unannounced at my home in Latham, New York, and demanded that my mother take me to the emergency room immediately. My mother was bewildered; she did not understand what was going on, but she bowed to the woman's demands.

At the emergency room, the CPS worker pointed at a mark on my body as evidence of physical abuse. The doctor said that it was a birthmark, so the case was closed.

Later, while my mother and I were living in China, the agent called and visited our house in America several times, asking my grandmother when we would return.

Were the CPS agents blind? Could they not see how good my mother was to me? In China, nothing like this would ever happen. Patients always have the right to disagree with doctors without facing any legal consequences, especially when the doctors themselves are not certain that their treatment will be one hundred percent effective. Patients already have enough worries weighing upon their hearts.

Anyone can clearly tell that my mother is an excellent mother after only a fraction of a moment. I have always been well-fed, well-dressed, and kept clean at all times. Above all, my happy disposition reflects the tender treatment my mother constantly and unconditionally supplies me.

I am taken from my mother for the first time

The first custody case, the first real taste of the horrifying ordeal my mother would be forced to endure, occurred when I was twenty-two months old at Boston's Floating Hospital for Children in Massachusetts. The hospital had given me aspirin on an empty stomach. The medicine caused severe side effects, including diarrhea and a fever of 104 degrees, not to mention drowsiness and a severe lack of energy. My mother insisted the staff stop administering aspirin. Instead, the hospital responded by sending her to court and immediately took her custody of me away.

Mother was ordered to undergo psychiatric evaluation. If she were to be judged incompetent, with psychological disorders, she would immediately lose parental rights permanently, and would not be allowed to see me for twenty years. Fortunately, she was found to be not only a very good mother but also a very smart one.

How could one psychological report determine whether my own mother could or could no longer *be* my mother? In such circumstances, when parents are found mentally incompetent, they will lose custody of their children. But if no disagreements between parents and doctors ever occur, mentally incompetent parents are still able to have children and maintain custody. People are not required to receive psychological evaluation to determine if they would be allowed to have children. But how come once parents disagree with doctors they will lose their parental rights if they are found to have psychological disorders?

Mother loses custody again

The state took me from my mother for the second time when I was seven years old.

The doctor at Newington Children's Hospital in Connecticut wanted to operate on six of my joints (my ankles, knees, and hips) in a single operation when he did not even have any medication to effectively control my inflammation. My health deteriorated because of his administering naproxen to me on an empty stomach. The custody case lasted five months, until my mother finally won me back. By then, I was all skin and bones and vomiting large amounts of blood.

The doctor ordered immediate surgery and claimed that it was in my best interests, without making any guarantees that it would be successful. But the surgery was not emergent. It was not a life-threatening situation where I had to have the surgery in order to live. The surgery could be done at a later time when I would be able to withstand both the surgery itself and the recovery that would follow. It was not just the surgery that I would have had to endure; I would have needed the physical and mental energy to endure the resulting pain and discomfort and had to go through extensive rehabilitation and therapy afterward. So receiving the surgery at that time was actually the worst option for me, not the best, as the doctor had claimed.

A close call

My mother almost lost custody of me for the third time when I was fourteen. I was in the emergency room for pneumonia and asthma. They had no relief for me, so we wanted to return home, but the doctor would not allow me to be discharged, in spite of the fact that he had no effective treatment for me. He immediately called CPS. Fortunately, the social worker from the hospital told my mother that she was free to bring me home, so we promptly left, and I got the much-needed rest. The CPS agent did not fail to show up at our condo later that day, but left when she saw that I was doing fine. I felt much better after I had slept. Some days later, the CPS worker checked on me again, and she saw that I had recovered considerably. This proves that my mother's decision was right all along.

When my mother read the medical report for this emergency-room visit and what the doctor had planned for me if I had stayed in the hospital, she was shocked to learn that, among his recommendations, I was to mainly receive a large amount of IV as "treatment." How could that treat asthma attack or relief my symptoms? It would just cause me more discomforts. All I needed was rest and effective treatment, and I would have gotten neither in the hospital if I had stayed. In experience, I could seldom rest in hospitals, for they performed unnecessary tidying-up tasks in the middle of the night and woke patients up to check their temperature.

I thanked God when I turned eighteen. I finally had freedom and that my mother would never get into trouble with CPS again. It had to have been my happiest birthday.

Finally, I am out of the unjust forces of the medical system. Nearly every time I visited a doctor, I felt apprehensive. There was always a chance that my mother would wrongly be accused of child abuse or medical neglect, and in turn, I would be trapped in the hospital to receive treatment I did not want.

I finally have the right, the freedom, to say no, without fearing the consequences.

Recent Custody Cases

The following pages contain brief outlines of some of the recent custody cases in America. They give you a general idea of what is happening in the medical system. Since this is not a reference book, I have only supplied a handful of cases, from the more general to the absurd. Any comments I have made are italicized. I did not comment on every case, for they speak for themselves.

Custody disputes between parents and the state are occurring more frequently, perhaps due to the fact that parents are now more educated in one way or another. With today's advanced technology and countless resources and opportunities, we have information right at our fingertips: easily accessible from the Internet, in print media sources such as magazines and newspapers, and so forth. And more and more parents are finding the will to fight back. Unfortunately, there are always parents who are alone, scared, or do not have the money or the ability (i.e., because of their own medical conditions, language barriers, and the like) to fight for justice. If all parents fought back, we would be inundated with these battles.

Most children whose parents have lost their parental rights have wound up in foster homes where total strangers are suddenly assigned to be their care and security. Putting children in foster homes endangers their lives. For instance, in a 1998 issue of the *Los Angeles Times*, reporter Tracy Weber discovered that "children under state protection in California group and foster homes are being drugged with potent, dangerous psychiatric medications, at times just to keep them obedient and docile for their overburdened caretakers."

On July 22, 2006, sixteen-year-old Abraham Cherrix lost his fight to follow his desired treatment for his Hodgkin's disease. A juvenile court judge ordered him to undergo the chemotherapy that had made him terribly ill. He was to report to the appointed hospital, Children's Hospital of the King's Daughters, in Norfolk, Virginia, on July 25 to receive the unwanted chemotherapy, and his parents were forced to give their legal written consent. The parents appealed. On July 25, Judge Glen A. Taylor from Accomack County Circuit Court lifted the orders of the juvenile court judge, and Abraham did not have to report as ordered to the appointed hospital. The judge also ended joint custody of Abraham between his parents and social services officials. Finally, the legal fight ended with victory in the teen's hand on August 16, 2006, when a judge decided that Abraham can follow the treatment of his choice.

On June 9, 2005, in Texas, Edward and Michele

Wernecke lost custody of their twelve-year-old daughter, Katie, who has Hodgkin's disease, because they disagreed with her doctor on the need for radiation treatment. The Werneckes had appealed in court to intercept the treatment and regain custody of their daughter. Katie lived in a foster home to receive the forced treatment neither she nor her parents wanted. She wanted to return home to her family. Child Protective Services told her that she would die if she did not receive the radiation treatment. CPS said that the parents could visit Katie only from noon to one in the afternoon. Seeing that Katie was so unhappy, which adversely affected the treatment's progress and her health, a judge ordered that Katie be returned to her parents.

On August 13, 2002, Corissa Mueller, an engineering graduate, sought routine medical care for her feverish five-week-old daughter, Taige, at St. Luke's Regional Medical Center. Within hours, the mother, accused of child neglect, lost custody of her infant. Doctors at St. Luke's told Mueller that there was a five percent chance Taige had contracted meningitis. They wanted to perform a lumbar puncture or spinal tap to test for the infection, and to inject Taige with antibiotics and steroids. Mueller thought Taige likely had the same cold the rest of the family had. She knew that spinal taps, steroids, and antibiotics carried risks, so she did not consent to the medical procedures. As advised over the telephone by Taige's naturopath, Dr. Karen Erickson, Mueller asked doctors to wait for initial lab results and until Dr. Erickson had a chance to speak with them before performing the lumbar puncture. A hospital nurse then called Child Protective Services. A detective announced that Taige was to be seized and removed to a shelter. Two police officers dragged Mueller down the hall and her baby was taken away. Doctors performed the spinal tap and administered antibiotics without Mueller's consent. They then diagnosed Taige with a cold. Mother and daughter were reunited two hours after their separation.

One February day in 2000, five-year-old Anthony Mitchell accidentally stepped on a nail playing with his brother. Anthony's mom, Pam Anderson, took him to the emergency room at Terre Haute's Union Hospital. While there, a mix-up of words led to the forced treatment of a negative disease. Anthony called the nail a needle, prompting the doctor to give him a dose of AZT, the DNA-chain terminator widely prescribed as an anti-AIDS drug, without performing any test, and called CPS. The doctor automatically thought that since they are black, they were using drugs (black-needle-drug-AIDS). Pam heard the doctor saying the f-word when he realized he had made a mistake, after speaking to the child's father over the telephone, but did not withdraw his diagnosis or treatment plan. CPS decided that Anthony should keep taking AZT, just in case he had stepped on an AIDS-infected needle, and ordered Pam to take Anthony to see a doctor at a clinic to see how he was doing on the medicine. Pam took her son to the clinic but did not put him on the drug. CPS called her, and armed police with dogs surrounded Pam's mother's house. Pam then got in touch with Deane Collie, executive director of Coalition for Medical Justice, who spoke with CPS. CPS then dropped the case, but warned that if Anthony were to come back with a positive HIV test within the next twelve months, Pam would be charged with felony criminal intent to harm.

On August 25, 2000, Authorities in New Mexico took away Anamarie Martinez-Regino, the three-year-old daughter of Miguel Regino and Adela Martinez, after a Presbyterian Hospital doctor claimed the child's obesity was life-threatening. The toddler was three times heavier and fifty percent taller than an average three-year-old, according to her doctor, Monika Mahal, who made the recommendation that she be removed from her parents' custody. For years, the parents had been seeking treatments for the girl's weight problem from many doctors performing plenty of tests and trying numerous diets to no avail. The state relinquished its legal custody of the girl in January 2001, but no doctor ever found out what was actually wrong with her. In January, Anamarie was losing weight under a treatment plan.

Anyone who eats at an excess must have a medical condition. Anyone who does anything excessively or inadequately, including sleeping, must have a medical disorder, and no one should be held responsible for such medical disorder. A normal person cannot possibly eat and eat and eat, without dying, because a healthy, normal, body is made by God to regulate itself. Otherwise, a person, especially one who is very wealthy, can eat and eat, and become ten thousand pounds. You cannot say that if a child is eating too much that their parent is neglecting them. A healthy person who is left in a room filled with food cannot and will not have the desire to stuff him or herself to the point that they will become hundreds of pounds overweight. What about those adults who weigh one thousand pounds? Whose fault is it when adults are severely overweight? Surely, there must be something abnormal in their bodies. But their parents will not be charged with neglect. Children have the same problem, but their parents are charged with neglect. You cannot blame a parent if the child has a medical condition that lets them under or overeat. Not only aren't the parents consoled during this hard time, they are instead being charged with neglect and have to be in fear of losing custody of their children. What about those odd "medical mysteries" that baffle doctors? In 2007, a fifteen-year-old girl hiccupped nonstop for five weeks; her hiccups stopped only when she was sleeping. She was hiccupping close to fifty times a minute. That is just one example of doing something excessively, but the doctors could not charge the parents with child abuse or neglect because, frankly, they could not imagine how the parents could do something to make the girl hiccup so frequently. And there are cases when people sneeze uncontrollably for an extended period of time, another medical mystery that doctors cannot charge parents with. But for something that has even the slightest "reasoning" on how the medical condition came to be or was still in existence, as in overeating, the doctor could charge the parents.

In 2000, a Columbus, Ohio, couple, Sherry and Paul Lipscomb, appeared in Franklin County Juvenile Court after they lost temporary custody on August 23, 2000, of their six-year-old transgender daughter, Aurora (physically born male, Zachary), after they enrolled her in first grade as a girl. Earlier that summer, a Cincinnati doctor diagnosed gender-identity disorder in the child, who had attended kindergarten at the same Westerville school as a boy. School employees and children services officials questioned the diagnosis, as well as the parents' refusal to force their daughter into gender stereotypes. The parents simply were trying to treat their child as the doctor had recommended. The unhappy Aurora was forced to dress and act like a boy in her foster home.

Aurora's case is different than the other cases listed here in mainly two ways:

1) The parents did follow a doctor's advice concerning their situation, but in this instance, it was the child protection agency that opposed the doctor's recommendation, and they decided to charge the parent.

2) It is not truly a medical case, but I wanted to include this to show what other absurdity occurs in the American legislative system.

People are born the way they are, and should be accepted the way they are. People should be able to be the way they feel most comfortable with. People are urged to not pretend to be someone they are not, so why is this child being treated differently? I believe that Aurora's parents have talked to her regarding her situation when they have even sought a doctor's advice. They did their best in their case, and the child protection agency should leave them alone to live a peaceful life. It was not as though the parents had forced her to feel like a girl. And it will not do anyone's harm that she feels like a girl. If this child is forced to be someone she did not feel comfortable about being, then she would not live a truly happy life.

In 1998, Valerie Emerson of Bangor, Maine, lost but won custody of her four-year-old HIV-positive son, Nikolas, after a judge ruled that her decision constituted not "medical neglect" but rather "informed choice." What was her decision? She refused a doctor's suggestion that Nikolas be part of an aggressive drug therapy trial, so the doctor reported her to the

Department of Human Services. Emerson's daughter died horribly taking AZT, she herself worsened on it, and Nikolas suffered terrible side effects while on the medication for ten weeks. She had stopped giving Nikolas AZT because she believed it would kill him, and felt that the new experimental drug cocktail would also harm him.

Not only was this mother brought to court to have unwanted treatment forced on her ill child, she was forced to consent to a dangerous experiment.

1997-1999: Tina Phifer, a New York City accountant and single mother, lost custody of her nine-year-old daughter, Amkia, and all visitation and contact rights, when she wanted to seek a second opinion for her daughter's treatment. She disagreed with doctors at Montefiore Hospital over the correct course of treatment for Amkia's gastrointestinal condition, which was first diagnosed as anemia, then as irritable bowel disease, then finally as ulcerative colitis. Phifer insisted that her daughter's health deteriorated only after doctors began treating Amkia with drugs she could not tolerate. She wanted to take Amkia to see other doctors, but the hospital promptly charged her with medical neglect. Tina said that for blood drawings, they had student interns who could not find veins and would stick her daughter four times, damaging her arms. She informed the hospital that Amkia was allergic to Amoxicillin in the past, but they still administered it to her. The court ordered that all communication between mother and daughter be audible to the social worker monitoring their weekly one-hour visits; she lost visitation and contact rights when she violated the order. Before the custody loss, Tina had taken Amkia to three different specialists in late 1996 and early 1997 to find the right diagnosis. Tina was also accused of "educational neglect" because she homeschooled Amkia, even though her education has been tested to be superior than other children her age. Amkia had lived in six foster homes in two years, among rats and roaches. After two years of the living nightmare, she was finally allowed to live with her mother again on a trial basis, but had to receive biweekly visits from child protection authorities.

Guilty until Proven Innocent

The state, doctors, and CPS need to know how to differentiate between child abuse and informed choice. Criminal suspects are innocent until proven guilty. Parents who refuse medical treatment for their children, on the other hand, are guilty of abuse or neglect until proven innocent. Criminal suspects keep parental rights to their children; parents who disagree with doctors lose child custody with a single command from the doctor.

When a parent freely seeks medical attention for his or her child, it should be clear that the parent wants what is best for the child, or else they would not have brought the child to the doctor in the first place. When the parent disagrees with what is medically recommended, that parent should have the right to a second, third, or fourth opinion.

If doctors are absolutely certain that their treatment can save a child in a life or death situation, then they should stress so with compassion, not by threat. If the initial attitude of a doctor is "If you don't listen to me, I'll report you to CPS," the doctor creates a hostile atmosphere wherein the parent feels trapped. It will consciously or unconsciously make the parent lose trust in the doctor.

When parents refuse doctors' recommendations, it is not logical to assume the parent is neglecting or abusing the child by choosing an alternative. For example, a mother brings her feverish eight-year-old child to a hospital to see what is wrong with the child. The child looks otherwise healthy and well-cared for. The mother then refuses the recommended treatment. Does that make her a child abuser? She could have ignored her child and not brought her child to the doctor.

Reasoning Using the Heart

No one should force anyone to do anything they do not want to do when it would not harm the life of someone else. They said they wanted the "best" for me, but how much love did they — the social workers and doctors — put into their job when they tore my mother and me apart?

When you help someone, the recipient should feel they are being helped. We did not feel like we were being helped. We felt like criminals.

What crimes do doctors commit on your child before they even lay a finger on your child? They force treatments on them. Children have no voice in treatments for their own bodies. This is mental assault and abuse that the medical system commits on the children, including those who are only one day shy from turning eighteen years of age. Children should have the right to decide for themselves, when they are competent and old enough to understand, what they want. If they are not competent, regardless of their age, then their closest guardian should help them to decide. Doctors should decide for them if the children or the children's guardian have specifically requested, or in the cases where children do not have any guardians, the doctors have to decide for them if they cannot decide for themselves. This is the only time when it is humane for doctors to speak for the children and make the final decision for any child's medical care and treatment.

Lack of Parental rights

Fact: Parents cannot disagree with medically recommended treatments, but they are asked to give their consent by signing their names on any consent forms before a medical procedure can be carried out.

• Why are parents asked to sign any consent form when no disagreement is allowed? Since it is mandatory for parents to say yes, it is therefore hypocritical for doctors to ask for their consent. Rather, doctors should initially inform parents the legal consequences of disagreeing with their recommendations, instead of shocking the parents by saying, "Ah ha, you said no, so you have lost custody." What kind of cruel trick is that? It is better to be unjust upfront than it is to be unjust behind people's backs.

• If parents cannot be trusted with their own children, why should a stranger be trusted?

• When parents have God-given parental rights of their children, they should have the right to exercise their rights, including speaking and deciding on behalf of their children. Since it is wrong and unlawful to force treatment on adults, it should be wrong and unlawful to force treatments on children, as it is violating the parent's wishes, for children belong to parents by the law of nature. The state should respect parental rights and therefore parents' refusal for treatment when the parents are loving and responsible.

• Can children choose to die in their parents' arms rather than in doctors' hands?

Parens Patriae "Parent of the Country" where the State Is the Guardian of Minors and Incompetent People

• If parens patriae is taken to its logical conclusion, the state should be held responsible if the child under their care dies.

• The state cannot declare itself as parens patriae and force their right onto being the father of minors and the mentally incompetent; we only have one Father. If no child or child's guardian has asked for the state to step in to be the child's "parent," then the state should not claim to be the child's father on their own.

• By tearing a child from their parents, the state is not considering how the forcible parent-child separation will affect the child.

• Children are not property, so the state should not claim to be their father without being asked to be so.

• Of course, it is perfectly admirable for the state to do their best in protecting the overall welfare of their citizens, but this protection should be done with love and care, not by force or power. It is not just the children that government needs to protect and care for. Every human being needs care and protection from others. The young, the old, and the sickly all need protection from abusive people or bad situations.

Unfair Double Standard

Fact: If a parent does the very best for their child and the child dies, the parent will be held responsible for the death. But if the doctor does the very best for the child and the child dies, the doctor will not be charged or held responsible for the death, unless the parents sue them. But what good is money to parents when their children have died or suffered tremendously?

• If the state wants to be fair and just, they should give the same rights to parents as they do to medical professionals. Parents should not be criminally prosecuted when they provided the very best care for their children, just like the doctors would not be criminally prosecuted when they did the very best for the children. If the state elects to charge the parents with child abuse or neglect despite their best efforts and intentions, then doctors should be charged as well when the children under their care die.

Life Matters

• Accidents and certain diseases are beyond human power to control or predict. Accidents strike every single person, young and old alike. By their very nature, accidents cannot be controlled or prevented.

There are accidents caused by nature, others, and ourselves. No one should be held responsible for an accident that cannot be controlled or prevented. Adults slip and fall or even die as a cause of accidents, and yet they or their parents are not to blame. But when the accidents are caused by a parent to a child, parents would be blamed. Since the average parent only wants the best for their child, they will not intentionally cause harm to the person they love.

• Life does not and cannot offer guarantees.

• Science and medicine are still trial and error, and cannot offer any guarantees.

• Since there are no contracts to sign and no guarantees for any treatment, then force should not be exerted on any parent who only wants the best for their child.

• Life is nothing to be gambled on.

• There are always disagreements in life and they are allowed, but refusing unwanted treatment is not allowed.

• Is forcing unwanted treatment the best thing to do?

• Leave nature alone. Animals have been caring for their offspring from the beginning of time...some offspring survive and some die. As long as parents are doing their best for their children, leave them alone. By tearing parents and children apart, you are disturbing the fundamental basis and balance of nature and what makes up the harmony of nature. The relationship between parents and their offspring is the most vital element in nature. Parents are the creator of life when they give birth to children; God bestowed this gift of power upon them.

State Vs. Parents

• The state vs. parents, who loves the child more?
• How can the state decide what is right for the child right away? They did not give birth to the child, nor have they reared the child.
• The state and parents: the classic case of the two women in King Solomon's story who fought over a child. The action of the fake mother revealed her true identity when she did not care for the welfare of the child when Solomon wisely thought of the idea to split the child in two so both women could have a piece of the child.
• The state should not treat every parent, every child, and every case the same way.

Do Doctors *Really* Know Best?

Should we do everything doctors tell us to do? Adults can refuse any treatment, but when it concerns a minor child, should we put our entire trust in the doctor?

Many people have the notion that doctors know best because of their medical training and experience. But do doctors *really* know best? The real question is: does *every* doctor know best? Since every individual is different, every doctor is different, and in turn, will have different opinions and treatment ideas for the same disease, illness, or condition.

Each doctor can say that their treatment is the best for the patient. Doctor A could say that Treatment 1 is the best option to treat your child's illness; Doctor B could insist that Treatment 2 is the best; Doctor C could recommend Treatment 3; while Doctor D could say the other doctors have the wrong diagnosis entirely! All of these doctors are professionally licensed and are experts in their field. So who is right?

Most importantly, even if the doctor knows best, knowing what is the best treatment for a particular illness is not the same as knowing what is the best for the patient. The patient and the disease are not one and the same. How would the doctor know for certain that the treatment is best for that patient even though the treatment is best for their illness itself? Just because a doctor recommends a specific medical treatment does not mean that the treatment is effective, guaranteed, harmless, or the best for the unique individual being treated.

We are often told how effective, in percentage, a treatment is for a certain disease, but do they tell us what the percentage is for how safe that treatment would be for a specific patient? No, because doctors do not know the answer to that information!

Would doctors be able to guarantee their treatment one hundred percent? Could they bet their own lives on it? If not, then how could they force their treatments on others? But even doctors can guarantee their treatments one hundred percent, they still should not exhort force on their patients. Not even God, our very Life-Giver, forces us to do anything, so why should fellow mortal creations act as though they are gods?

We must know that there is no one standard type of body. Every body is different, so every patient is different. Who can know what is best for that patient other than the patient or their parent or guardian? If everyone had the same body that would react in the same way, then and only then could doctors know what is best.

Since we have alternative treatments for most diseases, illnesses, conditions, it should be obvious to us that not every treatment is right for every patient. For example, some people are allergic to penicillin, so they need to take an alternative antibiotic. When adults visit their doctors, doctors often ask them, "How do you feel on this medicine?" If doctors know best, they would have not needed to ask this question. But because they cannot possibly know how the patient would feel while taking a certain drug, they need to depend on their patient's personal report to determine the next step to take—if the patient says that he has severe adverse reaction to the medicine, the doctor would then need to prescribe a different medicine. Hence, only the patient ultimately knows what treatment he can or cannot withstand. When adults have the right to follow any treatment of their choice or not follow any treatment at all, why should children be stripped of this right? The patient, regardless of age, should have the option to choose which doctor they want to see and which treatment they want to follow, just as we have the right to choose between any other option in life.

For some unique cases, to get to know a patient's illness, disease, or condition well, you need to stay with the patient on a day-by-day, minute-by-minute basis to familiarize yourself with their unique problems. In today's managed care health system, it is impossible for doctors to spend enough time with their patients to truly know them. Doctors may have a diagnosis for the illness, but there are always situations wherein the illness is not what the doctor has diagnosed despite the many similar symptoms. On the other hand, not having a diagnosis from a doctor for a patient's illness does not mean that patient is illness-free. Doctors need to know that they will not always make the correct diagnosis or prescribe the proper treatment, and that they need to listen to the patient because the patient knows their body and usually knows what's the best for them. There's a Chinese saying that if you have an illness long, you will automatically become a good doctor.

Law of Common Sense and Compassion

The parental rights issue is not just about laws and rights in black and white, it is about being humane, of having human compassion and human understanding, along with common sense, which has become very uncommon.

Hence, the root cause of the injustice in this parental rights matter is the lack of common sense and compassion. When we do not have enough of these precious commodities, we will face problem at every corner of our lives. To fix this problem concerning the God-given rights of parents, we must dig up its roots, replant them in a rich soil and fertilize them with abundant compassion, understanding, and common sense.

Here, I would like to supply a few pointers to get us start heading in the right direction:

First, we need to respect and honor other people's wishes, customs, and cultural differences, even when we do not understand them.

Put yourself in other people's shoes. How would you feel if you were they and enduring what they are going through? How would you feel if complete strangers force you to do something for your own body that goes against your wishes?

Second, we must not force anyone to do anything they do not want to do. It's a violation against the sanctity of the family when you force parents to do something to their children when they strongly disagree with you. A doctor can insist that their treatment is extremely important. The doctor can get on his knees and beg, but dialing CPS when the parents refuse to comply is cruel, ruthless, and heartless.

Lastly, we need to understand that the patient must have a significant level of belief and faith in the treatment and must invest a significant amount of effort to receive the full benefit of the treatment and to properly recover from any pain and discomfort. Spiritual health is as important, and sometimes more important, than physical health. A person has to feel comfortable receiving a certain treatment in order to experience the complete benefit of the treatment.

Compassion and common sense

Love and common sense are the ingredients that make any person knowledgeable about any disease and the needs of the patient. If you lack these two most important elements, even if you have all the knowledge in the world, you will not be a good caregiver at all. That is why we have faced so many problems with doctors and officials.

They may be experts in their fields, but they do not know anything about my needs when they lack love and common sense. My mother has both love and common sense in full abundance, so she is the smartest doctor I have ever met.

Love and common sense are the best elements you can bring with you to your practice, to your patients, or in everyday living, for that matter. Always have an open heart and ears to listen to the voices of your patients and their caregivers. You may not fully understand their needs or problems, but respect them. Do your best in accommodating their needs and requirements. Do not just give them your treatment, give them your heart. Do not just use your brain, use your heart more often. By doing so, you are setting good examples for others, including your fellow professionals. See that your patients are happy, not just healthier. Life is all about happiness, being there for one another, and being life smart.

Patients do not need just your knowledge; patients need your love and common sense even more. A doctor who is skilled and lacks compassion and common sense does more harm than good.

Laws Vs. People

Can we blame everything on doctors for making parents and their ill children miserable? No, we cannot. Just like a bad math teacher who gives his students poor math instructions and methods to solve problems, the government gives doctors poor laws to follow regarding parental refusal of medical treatment. Doctors would not be able to unjustly threaten parents if these laws did not exist. If no doctors follow the laws, then the laws will be of no use.

What parents actually experience solely depends on each doctor. Some doctors will use any excuse to take advantage of the unjust forces, while others do not touch these laws unless absolutely necessary—they instead use common sense and compassion to deal with their cases. Fortunately, not every doctor will take away a parent's custody after the parent says no to a medical treatment; otherwise, I cannot imagine how many custody cases there would be in America

Hence, the main culprit is the American government. If lawmakers had created more sensible laws, we would not encounter this kind of injustice in the first place. Luckily, as with most mistakes and errors in judgment, there are solutions to this problem. First, the lawmakers must accept that the laws are unjust. Here is where we face the greatest obstacle—how many people will admit they are wrong? How many can actually realize what they did, no matter how well-intended, was wrong?

After overcoming this challenge, the lawmakers can review and rewrite the laws to include the ingredients of common sense and compassion. When reforming these laws, they need to keep in mind that loving parents want the best for their child. Disagreeing with a recommended treatment does not make them guilty of child abuse, nor does it justify separating them from their children.

I have written my own set of laws, which I named *Shirley's Law*. It addresses the main points of parental rights in children's medical care, and is on page forty-five in this book.

It is often harder to fight human nature than it is to fight the laws. After all, laws are created by people. And it is especially hard to fight people who use unjust laws as weapons.

Wake Up, America!

Taking away a parent's custody is not a one-size-fits-all solution. Do doctors really think that by tearing a parent and their child apart will fix the child's medical condition? A parent who actually abuses her child should not only lose her parental rights but should also be locked behind bars. But just because a very small number of parents abuses children does not mean that the vast majority of parents should receive the same criminal treatment.

The medical system acts godly without God's compassion and understanding. In truth, it is an insult to God to say that American doctors act like God when, in fact, they do not act any way close to God, for God is Love and Understanding Himself, and does not decide for anyone at all.

Uncle Sam is too involved in our private lives and personal decisions. When parents want help, they will ask for it, but they will never ask for this kind of "help" where you "help" only by taking away their children. Parents need support during hard times of coping with their children's illnesses and finding the right treatment, not being accused of child abuse or medical neglect. What kind of example does the government give to its citizens when they force "help" on others? Would they welcome this kind of help for themselves?

So for once, wake up, open your hearts. Have a bit of love in your medical prescription.

When you, doctors, ask yes or no, parents should have the right to say no. When you ask them to sign the consent form, realize they have the right to refuse. And when you tell them to follow your treatment, allow them to seek a second opinion.

If you sincerely want to be helpful, start helping by preventing and stopping abuse in places that really need your help: hospitals, nursing homes, schools, foster homes, and the like; not in the homes of loving parents. If you could focus your energy on those places, society will truly thank you for it.

We want the state, doctors, and CPS to be remembered for what they did *for* the children, not what they did *to* them.

Shirley's Law

Let us turn our country into a true nation run by the people for the people.

Amendment XXVIII

Parents shall have the right to disagree and refuse treatments recommended by doctors for their minor-aged children. A minor-aged child is defined as being under eighteen years of age. The state shall not take away a parent's custody of their child over treatment disagreements and refusals. No parent of a minor-aged child shall be prosecuted or be held responsible for uncontrollable diseases, accidents, and deaths when the parent has done their utmost best in providing care for their child. The state shall treat cases in accordance with the unique needs of each case. Parents shall have the right to seek and exercise alternative treatments other than the ones recommended by their child's physician. Parents shall have the right to protect, defend, and speak for their minor-aged children.

Parents, What Should You Do When It Happens to You?

• **First, do not panic! Remain calm and faithful. Remember, when you hold justice in your hand, you should win. Do not be afraid.**

My mother knew that God was looking after both of us, so she put all of her faith in Him and let Him help her win both custody cases and the battles against other false accusations. She knew she had grounds and her reasoning would prevail.

• **Get the media's attention. Call the local newspapers (where the case is taking place) and explain your problem, and ask them to interview you for their publication. Start locally, then call up the major media. Usually, when the local paper comes out with your news, your story will spread to other media outlets.**

Right after she lost custody of me the second time, my mother called the *Hartford Courant* as soon as she returned to her apartment. Shortly after the newspaper reported the case, major media outlets began picking up the story. She appeared on local TV channels, then later on CBS *This Morning* show with Paula Zahn, and numerous national newspapers reported her case. The first custody case did not receive any media attention because only a Chinese newspaper knew about it, so it did not spread to English media. Be certain to include English media outlets among your press contacts.

• **Find a lawyer who is well-known.**

My mother had George Athanson as her lawyer for her second custody case. Big names can do the trick. She was on her own throughout her first custody case.

• **Contact any advocate groups, the American Civil Liberties Union, senators, etc.**

Although my mother did not do this (America was quite a foreign country to her and she did not know many organizations), I advise you to contact as many of these groups as possible. The more people who know about your problem, the more help you will get (even if it is just advice or consolation), and the more noise will be made.

• **Remain calm throughout your custody case.**

When my mother fought for my life, she held no grudges or bitterness. Instead, she focused on her goal—saving my life. If she harbored any negative feelings (i.e., hatred for the doctors and the government), her mind would have been too crowded to have room for clear focus and determination. She was still very friendly toward those who did her wrong. Even today, she holds no grudges and is in complete inner peace.

• **Finally, fight until you win.**

My mother stopped fighting only when

she won the custody cases.

Objections To My Argument

I have collected the most common opposing thoughts I have received on the issue of parental rights in children's medical care from those who agree with the current laws and who oppose my thoughts, and I have addressed them with my answers and viewpoints.

Sometimes I get responses from opposing parties, such as "You need to forget and forgive" and "You're angry about what happened to your mom" and the like. First of all, opposing anything in life does not mean that the opponent is angry. If something is wrong, it is wrong. I will not say something is right when I strongly believe it is wrong. And I especially will not remain silent and let what is wrong continue. Everyone has the right to his or own views. Disagreeing with something does not mean that one is harboring anger or is less objective. People oppose my thoughts and I allow them to. I do not tell someone, "You are angry" just because she or he opposes me.

Above all, being angry is not the point. So what if I *were* angry? That would not mean anything. By claiming that I am angry when I oppose America's laws, you are diverting attention from the real problem. If you oppose someone's opinions and views, keep comments about their feelings and emotions out of the discussion. Instead, focus on the subject in question; do not change the focus by commenting on insignificant things, such as the opponent's feelings.

I wrote this book not to vent about what happened to my mother and me personally, but for the entire American society to 1) make parents aware of the problems that could affect them and warn them of the legal consequences if they disagree with a medically recommended treatment, 2) to advocate for parents, and finally, 3) to put an end to this injustice. This book cannot affect the past legal and civil treatment of my mother and will not affect me now that I am over the age of eighteen. And, no, I am not advocating this issue just because we went through the ordeal; I am advocating for parents because many parents have undergone the same difficulty. It is, however, how I became an advocate.

Forgiving someone does not mean that you are forgetting; it means you can recall the situation without any grudge. I hold no grudge to those who did my mother and me wrong, but will not forget what they did to us. The purpose of this book is to prevent history from repeating itself. I lived in the past and personally experienced the wrongdoing, so I am able to come out of it and inform others that what has been happening is wrong and that we should reform the laws to make them better. Even after all the fear my mother had experienced at the hands of our nation's medical and legal systems, she holds no grudge or bitterness. Having anger in our souls will not help us in any way; it will not change anything or make any situation better. We choose to move forward with an open heart and with the courage to speak out. We want the best for the community. We see that the current laws could be better for people, so we have the responsibility as citizens to speak up. Let me add here that I am one who simply remembers things — the good, the bad, and the ugly. The past is a part of my life. Why should I forget what I have experienced, felt, and learned? Everything I do this minute will become my past the next minute. The past is not a blur to me and should not be one, either; it is as important as any other part of my life. Otherwise, what I learn today will all become a waste tomorrow.

In one sense I am actually thankful for having gone through the ordeal. Otherwise I would not be advocating this issue. I believe that one has to taste the ordeal to truly understand what it is like and to have full sympathy for those who have experienced it. When you can see or hear and you say to a blind or deaf person, "Oh, I know how you feel," that would not be true. You could not really know how it feels without going through blindness or deafness yourself. Just because you fumbled around the room in darkness does not mean that you have experienced blindness.

In a big way, I can understand why people oppose my views the way they do: they have never experienced what we, and a slew of other parents and children in America, have gone through. They cannot understand the extent of the injustice and horror involved.

After you have experienced this injustice, then come back to me and oppose my thoughts. After the state takes your child away from you when you disagree with a doctor's poor medical decision, then tell me that the doctor and state have simply made a mistake.

Historians research and write down everything that went wrong and everything that went right in our past. We take history classes to see what went wrong or right, and why it happened the way it did, so that we can learn how not to repeat the same mistakes, errors, and offenses. We live and learn, and we can only learn from the past, the errors people made in the past, so that we can live a better present.

Typical objections

1) Nobody can make us go see a doctor.

Unfortunately, any parent can be forced to take their child to the doctor. My mother was forcibly escorted to the emergency room by an unannounced CPS worker when I was an infant. If parents do not take their children to see doctors when forced to by CPS, they risk losing their custody rights.

2) Parents don't always know best.

Parents may not have book knowledge, but they have parental and life knowledge, and they are the only group of people on Earth that have been given the right by nature to care and look after children. Does that not mean much? I stress here, if we must choose between doctors and parents to best care for the children, it is better to choose parents. A line has to be drawn somewhere.

3) We can't let children suffer for their parents' poor choices.

Are children not the victims of martyrdom when doctors force treatments on them?

4) Doctors are more qualified than parents to make medical decisions.

Out of the one hundred doctors graduating from the same class with the same degree, ten percent may be excellent doctors; seventy percent may be average skilled; and the rest of them may be not that smart at all. All one hundred of those doctors are well-educated, holding the same degree from the same college. Should we listen to all of them?

Do all of them know best? Plus, as every individual is different, each doctor is different, so will recommend different treatment for the same disease. Flip back to the chapter in this book titled *Do Doctors* Really *Know Best?*

5) Doctors are human, too; they can make errors in judgment.

So you would call forcing unwanted or unnecessary — and sometimes harmful — treatments on children a mistake? You would call forcing a parent to give his or her legal consent a mistake, too? And I suppose opposing a parent's disagreement is a mistake as well. Well, even if they are mistakes, what do you think these mistakes cost parents and children? What if my mother had lost custody of me the first time?

6) Doctors are only acting in children's interests.

Are not the parents only acting in children's interests by defending them?

If doctors and the state really want to protect the children's interest, then they should ask what the children want. They should not assume that the children want the same thing they want.

Not a single doctor had ever asked me what I thought when I was a minor. They never consulted me about their treatment plans for me. At age seven, I knew I did not want the surgery; when I was fourteen, I did not want to stay in the hospital. Did the doctors know that? They did not even ask me. I doubt that I was the only child who had no voice. Minors have no voice, so how do doctors and CPS workers and the state know what the children want when they do not listen to them? Plus, does the state really protect the children's interest by taking them away from their parents?

The state claims that speaking for the children is "best" for them, but parents have God-given rights to speak for their children. Decision-making, especially regarding medical care and treatment, is a family process. Adults have the right to talk it over with their family, but children do not hold the same right. Not even the children's family has the right. Instead, all rights fall into the hands of the state.

7) Society is obligated to make every effort to prevent child abuse.

Yes, without harming innocent parents. It is better to let a guilty person go free than imprison a single innocent person. If you want to prevent one child abuse by affecting the rest of the parent population, then it is just similar to war, where you catch the bad guys by harming a great amount of civilians.

A line should be drawn somewhere. You have to know where to stop. Catching bad parents is extremely important, but so is respecting the sovereignty of loving parents.

8) Some parents truly do abuse or neglect their children.

Some doctors lie in their medical reports and even molest their patients. But just because some doctors are bad does not mean that every doctor is bad. Likewise, just because some parents are abusive does not mean every parent is a child abuser. The government should treat each case according to its unique needs and circumstances, instead of separating parents and children every time medical disagreements arise.

Excerpts of Personal Experiences

The following pages contain excerpts from my autobiography, *The Revelation of a Star's Endless Shine*, on my mother and my personal experiences with the injustice of the American medical system, including the two custody cases we had to endure and pray for victory.

Most of the names used in the excerpts have been changed to protect the individuals' privacy. Please note that my mother's name was Yi before she became an American citizen and changed her name to Juliet.

The excerpts are straight from my autobiography, so some parts may be confusing to you since you might not have read the entire book and may not understand the complete role of every character. Overall, the excerpts are comprehensible, as they are focused on specific time periods in my life. Please note that I have left the chapter headings in place.

The first custody case starts on page fifty-eight, the second custody case begins on page eighty-two, and the excerpt of our close call starts on page 135.

First Custody Case

Excerpted from Chapter Ten

At the beginning of October, a few days after Yi started piroxicam, Dr. Robinson recommended a pediatric rheumatologist located in Boston—Boston's Floating Hospital for Children at New England Medical Center.

"And there is another doctor from Columbia University in New York City," he further said. "But Dr. Schelling, the doctor in Boston, had written a book about arthritis."

"I think I will take her to see Dr. Schelling then," decided Yi. Before going there, Yi called up the hospital and told them of Shirley's situation. Then an appointment was made for the third of the month to see Dr. Schelling.

***

So as not to exert any pressure on Shirley's body to cause more pain, Yi carefully dressed her up appropriately. Yi strapped Shirley in the seat before Al started the car for the long drive to Boston from Latham. Yi and Shirley simultaneously let out a pair of yawns as Yi focused through the misty late morning.

"Finally here," Yi said under her breath when afternoon had arrived.

Al and Yi brought Shirley to the waiting room and sat down to wait. Moments later, they were called into a room, and a woman, wearing a white uniform, walked in. "Hi, I'm Dr. Persse," the woman introduced herself. Yi returned her greeting.

"Where is Dr. Schelling?" inquired Yi.

"Dr. Schelling will come to see Shirley later." The three seated themselves, Dr. Persse with her notepad in one hand, with the other poised above the clean sheet of paper.

Yi began to explain Shirley's history and her hopes for an effective treatment. "Shirley had been taking aspirin before, but she had very bad reactions on the medicine. Will you have other medicine?"

"Have her stay in the hospital and we'll see what we can do for Shirley," Dr. Persse answered.

"Shirley is currently on piroxicam, which is prescribed by the doctor in China," Yi said further. Dr. Persse scribbled all the information down, without saying more than a few words.

Accordingly, Shirley was admitted in the Boston's Floating Hospital for Children on the twenty-ninth of October. Yi and Shirley lived in a room in the hospital they had provided for them. Yi had high hopes this time. She thought that it would bring promising results to help Shirley. She had stopped piroxicam after giving it to Shirley for a mere week when she did not find it improving

Shirley any. Dr. Persse had explained that physical therapy would help. Yi waited to meet Dr. Schelling for the first time, wondering what the doctor might be like. Shirley did not see Dr. Schelling on the appointed day, so Yi had only conversed with Dr. Persse.

But a hopeful dream was shattered into pieces of sharp glass. It did not need to take long for Yi to learn that they had stumbled into a rose bush. It looked like such a perfect plan at first sniff, never aware of the thorns underneath.

On the very first day, the nurse administered a large dose of aspirin for Shirley. Yi was taken aback. She had informed the doctor that aspirin did not work from day one. But Yi had to give it another try; it was a Hobson's choice. If it did not work, she thought, they would stop and try something else. Let them find out for themselves.

Shirley's health became worse and worse on aspirin, with the same symptoms as the first time, but on a much more serious scale. The medication was given to Shirley on an empty stomach each time.

Even though the adversity was apparent, the hospital ignored it and simply continued administrating aspirin. Yi could not believe her eyes. How could they continue when the facts were clear?

Yi talked to them about it and requested that they give Shirley some other medication, but they only shook their heads.

"She has to continue to take it. It is the only way," they replied. They gave her the same response every time she asked them.

If aspirin is the only medicine they will give Shirley, how come I need to have Shirley hospitalized? Yi questioned herself. She could have given it to Shirley in the comfort of their own home.

By now, Shirley was running a high fever, and was in extreme pain day and night. But in spite of the ordeal, Shirley still laughed at any chance she got. She glowed when her eyes rested upon the animal pictures around the hospital.

Meanwhile, they gave Shirley physical therapy on a regular basis. Even when Shirley was constantly running a high fever of 104 and in great pain with red and swollen joints, physical therapy would still continue. Yi was outraged by their poor action. Yi asked them to discontinue with the therapies. It would only bring harm if done under such conditions. But they would not listen.

"I read an article in a medical book that states that under high fever and when the joints are in great pain, physical therapy should not be done," Yi told them.

Dr. Persse replied, "They provide wrong information in books sometimes."

Yi gave them a definite, "no" to the continuation of aspirin and physical therapy. Plus, the baby could not get any sleep in the hospital; whenever she fell asleep, they woke her up for physical therapy.

"If you do not cooperate with us, we will send you to court," they threatened. And true to their words, they sent over Louis Small, a hospital lawyer, who gave Yi the same message.

"Okay, I will wait and see how the treatment will turn out," Yi told them. Yi had no one to help her, and certainly she did not want to cause any problems. All she wanted was for Shirley to receive good care. Did they not understand that? Or did they just need reminding?

The second day, however, the torture of Shirley resumed. Yi, who could no longer bear the ill treatment, yelled to them next day, "Okay, I will see you in court!" She could not and would not stand there like a frightened, mistreated dog when she clearly saw that the hospital was making Shirley's condition worse. Like a mother lioness, she would rise and fight for her daughter's life till the utmost end, and only until victory would be achieved for Shirley.

Accordingly, a Care and Protection Order was obtained on November 5 from the Boston Juvenile Court. Before the court session, they asked if Yi would like to have an interpreter. And Yi nodded. "My English is not good."

Once the proceedings began, they immediately took away Yi's custody of Shirley upon an unhesitant decision. At the same time, the hospital had increased the aspirin dosage from 75 mg to 120 mg a day for Shirley. They also enforced physical therapies twice daily and occupational therapy once daily.

Yi desperately needed to win, not for her own sake, but Shirley's. She knew that Shirley's health would deteriorate on a significant level under the rugged care.

"Mrs. Cheng gave Shirley medication without the supervision of a doctor," was the hospital's accusation they brought against Yi in court, not the real reason of the case: Yi's refusal of their medical care. They had known that Shirley had taken piroxicam from day one. Yi had told them of this when she explained Shirley's history before arriving in Boston. It was the reason why Yi had brought Shirley here; because none of the medications worked.

Despite this terrifying moment, Yi was calm and composed, and her eyes exhibited exuberant courage and stamina. Her interpreter was both a white student going for his doctoral degree in anthropology and a professor at Harvard University. He kindly translated what was said. Yi was grateful to him, as he was compassionate to her ordeal. Immediately, Yi was forbidden to stay with Shirley in the same room, but was allowed to visit Shirley.

"I will come to see Shirley whenever I get the chance," her interpreter, Samuel, told Yi. Yi was comforted a great deal by his kind offer.

That night after they returned from court, Samuel visited Shirley. "She is so adorable!" he exclaimed as soon as his eyes fell upon the baby. He gaped with much admiration. He could not take his eyes off such an amazing creature.

Since Yi could not sleep in the same room with Shirley, she went around the hospital on many nights, seeking a room to stay in for the night. They frequently changed rooms for her as if treating a vagabond. She sometimes waited till one or two in the wee hours of the morning to obtain a key to a room where she was to sleep. Still, on top of it all, Yi would remember to go to Shirley's room to feed Shirley a bottle of milk every morning at two, for it was the time when the hospital gave Shirley aspirin on an empty stomach. Yi was often startled by a sudden booming voice behind her, ordering, "Stop! Shirley is not allowed to drink at night." If it had not been for Yi, Shirley's stomach would suffer from severe bleeding. Yi would not let them stop her from caring for her own daughter, especially when she knew they were wrong in their actions.

"Mrs. Cheng, you're not allowed! I am going to write a report to the judge," they threatened.

"You go ahead," Yi fired back. Unflinching, Yi never stopped coming.

"You *still* did not go home Yi? You are exhausted!" commented Samuel one day when he was visiting Shirley. They had ran into each other several times when he and his wife were visiting Shirley. "You need to go home now." Yi only shook her head weakly.

Only for a few times, Yi, being overly exhausted in the hospital without any sleep, went home in Latham for one or two days. Shirley needed a strong mother to support her, so Yi needed to get some of her physical strength back to withstand the ordeal. Once, when Yi returned to the hospital, she could not find Shirley in her room. Frantic, Yi asked them where Shirley was. They told her that Shirley was quarantined because she had the common cold.

When Yi at last found Shirley, she was shocked to see the state Shirley was in. The sleepy Shirley sat alone on a bed; mucus from her nose ran into her mouth, her unchanged diaper was filled with her feces, and she was unclean from head to toe. Upon seeing this, Yi rushed over, picked up Shirley, and went to the washing room to bathe her.

"Mrs. Cheng, stop," they ordered. "You cannot give her a bath, she has a cold."

"That's why I must give her a bath. Shirley needs it. It can make her better," Yi fought them off and continued on her way.

The same picture was replayed and the same scene reenacted every time Yi returned from Latham. Each time, Yi only spent a mere day in Latham; and Yi only had left a few times during the whole span of the ordeal. How could she leave Shirley entirely under the hospital's supervision when they could not even properly care for Shirley for only one single day? Not only was it a physical torment, but also a calvary for both Yi and Shirley.

Chapter Eleven

Days slowly dragged on painfully, with each step more agonizing than the one before it, while they carried the crosses on their backs. Yi struggled to maintain her sang-froid to endure their harsh life. Each day ticked on with Yi always fighting to get the chance to feed Shirley at two in the morning in spite of the hospital's forbiddance. Yi saw that her daughter's condition was getting worse by the minute during the duration of the hospital stay. Because of Shirley's severe crippling disease, she would be prone to contracting uveitis. A split lamp examination of her eyes was performed under sedation and revealed no evidence of asymptomatic uveitis.

The most tortuous time for Shirley during the stay was receiving the therapies sessions. She was required to sit on the playroom's floor daily for at least three hours in the afternoon. When it was nap time for other children, the playroom supervisor would always carry Shirley to the playroom, many times waking her. Thus, the sleepy Shirley could not sleep, but had to sit alone on the cold, tile floor, sometimes with a few toys. The hospital said that Shirley needed to be active because of her arthritis. *So, this is called physical therapy, being on the cold floor to sit by herself for three hours a day?* thought Yi, incredulously.

Once, Shirley did not sleep the entire night because of her usual pain. At last, at six in the morning, her eyes closed. But instantly, she was awakened to drink two ounces of water, for they did not want to get her dehydrated since she was always lacking an appetite, so she could not receive enough nourishment.

"Can't you let her sleep? She didn't sleep the whole night," Yi pleaded. Her only answer was a definite shake of their heads. Yi argued with them. But it was too late to do anything; Shirley was already awake.

On top of everything, Yi had to attend court sessions and had to endure the false accusations made by the hospital. "Mrs. Cheng has a psychological disorder, high level of anxiety, and she force-feeds Shirley," they also accused. They asked that Yi be evaluated by a hospital psychiatrist. During all the court sessions, Yi could not speak for herself and tell them her side of the story—no one was providing any help to speak for her. Her court-appointed lawyer never spoke one word for her during any court session, for he did not know the full spectrum of the story. Once, the judge asked him some questions, and the lawyer only shrugged his shoulders and shook his head.

Samuel had spent an entire night, without any sleep, writing a long and detailed report on her case, hoping it would help. After writing the report overnight, he had given it to her the following noon right after he completed the detailed fourteen pages of typed report.

Unlike what Samuel and Yi had hoped, no one paid attention to the report. Yi was not sure who else had read it besides herself. She had read the report with trouble, for the English words were hard. But she was able to understand the content of the document. She read with a pounding heart and a shocked soul when she got to the part where Samuel had listed what the hospital psychologists had reported:

"Shirley was carried around by her parents and when approached by hospital staff, she would cry and hide her face. This behavior did not decrease with familiarity with staff."

"Shirley will at times display a great deal of anger during the therapy sessions, and refused to cooperate with the physical therapist. The behavior problem is exacerbated by the presence of her mother."

"Separation of parents and child during the course of this admission has been exceedingly difficult."

The statements made by the psychologists struck Yi with total disbelief. The spontaneous response of the twenty-two-month-old baby, in constant pain from the crippling disease, should not be taken as any signs of a dysfunctional family. Above all, Shirley had been separated from Yi by force. Should such reactions by an infant be taken as a family pathology?

Yi knew that she must win the battle. *There is no other way*, thought Yi. *This is the battle against evildoers.* She would permanently lose the custody to her own child if she lost. *Win, I must*, she thought with resolve. But how could their icy hearts listen to her reasons?

One day, Yi was called to the stand during a court session. At long last, the moment she had been waiting for finally arrived. She could now speak for herself. The judge asked Yi several questions. It was the moment she had been waiting for.

"Why did you give a prescription medication to Shirley without the supervision of a doctor?" asked the judge.

"The medication was prescribed by the doctor in China. So, I put Shirley on it. But she was only on it for one week. I did not know about the medical law of America. I will not give Shirley any medication without the doctor's supervision from now on," answered Yi.

The judge continued, "Why do you refuse to see this psychiatrist? If you give me a good reason, I will find a different psychiatrist for you."

"Everyone in the hospital says I have psychological disorders. This psychiatrist is from the same hospital, who already has bias toward me, so I think that she will naturally most likely say the same thing about me," Yi reasoned.

"Okay, very good, I'll make some phone calls right now," stated the judge. "Would you like a Chinese or an American psychiatrist?"

"I prefer a Chinese or an Oriental psychiatrist," answered Yi.

"There are no Chinese psychiatrists, but we have a Korean." He reported after he returned.

Yi nodded. "That is fine. Thank you, Your Honor."

"Okay, I appoint this psychiatrist for you." The people below listened on. At that moment, Yi knew that she was on the road to victory. It was the first and crucial step of the battle. She had scored a large point by having the judge appoint a different psychiatrist.

I didn't understand that in court, they would charge me with privately giving Shirley this medicine which I had brought back with me from China, thought Yi. *I find it strange that at the time when I openly conveyed this information to Dr. Persse, she didn't stop me, and later, used this honest admission as an accusation against me. I realized how accurate Samuel's report was regarding the case.* In it, he stated:

"Having taken hasty legal steps to secure custody, and continued to argue a hard line using problematic psychological concepts, the hospital had committed two levels of error..."

"...the pattern of multiple resort and individual initiative in providing medication is a very familiar one in China and indeed in all areas of the world where professional medicine has not achieved such total and absolute control over the pharmaceutical and medical markets."

"The first responsibility of the healer in the clinical encounter is sympathetically and fully to elicit the patient's background and explanatory model for the problem involved."

"Decision-making is a family process, complex disagreements may occur between family unit and physicians and nurses, before rushing off to court, and ruthlessly depriving the parents of their ancestral grounds for meaningful existence."

The judge's voice interrupted Yi's thoughts. "Don't worry, every afternoon at three I have a high level of anxiety myself," the judge comforted Yi with a smile toward the end of the session. Among the handful of audience listening to the session, most were doctors from the hospital. A few laughs rang throughout the courthouse. The psychiatric evaluation was scheduled to get underway.

"I would not speak as well in Chinese if I had stayed in China for only five years," the Massachusetts State social worker, Melinda, said to Yi when meeting her after the court session. "You did a really good job. You spoke very well, pointing out things very clearly."

"Thank you. I have the reason, the truth. The truth is on my side," said Yi.

"If you are found to have psychological disorders from the psychological evaluation, you'll permanently lose custody of Shirley and you won't be allowed to see her for twenty years."

***

Yi held Shirley in her arms outside her room. Yi gently rocked her to and fro, trying to sooth the crying child who was in pain. Yi lifted her head and noticed a figure coming their way. An Oriental lady with dark short hair came into Yi's view.

The woman walked toward Yi. "Are you Mrs. Cheng?"

"Yes. So, you are the psychiatrist."

"Yes," the doctor answered with a formal nod.

"Please come in," Yi showed her into the room. Yi gently placed Shirley into the stroller. Shirley continued to cry.

"Why don't you carry her?" asked the psychiatrist.

"Today's a bad day for you to come to examine us. My daughter is running a high fever of 103. She has been crying the whole day long. I don't know if I am allowed to carry her or not. They said I overprotect her, so I don't want to appear as though I am overprotective." Yi was unsure what to do. Should she carry

Shirley, and look as if she was being overprotective? Or should she ignore Shirley? Would that look as if she was neglecting her?

"Go ahead," said the psychiatrist, "carry her," Grateful, Yi picked Shirley up and held Shirley in her arms for the remaining of the examination. Yi was expecting a Chinese interpreter to come that day, but she did not show up. The psychiatrist began to ask Yi questions that required only common sense, like questions that were asked on IQ Tests. The examination lasted for exactly an hour.

"I will tell you the result now," the doctor said, "not only don't you have any psychological disorders, but you are also very smart. Plus, you are a very good mother. And I'm going to write this in the report to the judge."

From that moment, Yi knew she would get Shirley back. No words could describe her happiness.

Yi's thoughts rewound to the time before the custody case began. Dr. Robinson had recommended two doctors for Shirley: one from New England Medical Center in Boston, and the other one from Columbia University in New York City. He had told Yi the doctor in Boston had written a book about arthritis. Therefore, Yi had chosen Boston over New York. Then once Yi lost the custody, Yi was not allowed to bring Shirley to see Dr. Robinson, for he was not a pediatric rheumatologist. The judge had told Yi earlier that she was allowed to take Shirley to Columbia University. But Yi thought it would be too much for Shirley, and besides, they all had the same treatment. So, why have Shirley travel unnecessarily? Yi had also fervently believed that the hospital was still doing their hardest in Shirley's best interest. They would still help. Yi had even given Dr. Persse two scarves, never expecting that the doctor could so cruelly bring the fallacious charges against her. She had clung to that belief, and decided to stay in Boston. Yi sighed as she thought back. She had made a mistake. Only after she remained did the hospital accuse her of having psychological disorders.

Soon afterward, on December 20, Yi was allowed to take Shirley home at Latham following a Boston Juvenile Court appearance, but she still did not have full custody of Shirley. A full hearing was scheduled for a date several weeks later. Yi was ordered to bring Shirley to see the doctor at the Boston's Floating Hospital for Children on February 5 for a follow-up. Having her baby back was the best Christmas present she could ever wish for.

Yi, holding the bundle of treasure in her arms, left the hospital. Even after all the ordeal of the false accusations and the unnecessary physical and emotional torments, Yi did not hold any grudges toward anyone. It was futile to have vengeance and anguish upon her heart. She was grateful that she had won the case — she *knew* she had won the case even though she had not been told. It was God's help and the divine will of His plans.

At that time, Yi had learned that Dr. Persse had just had her first child and planned to depart for Canada. How could one woman bring such misery upon a whole family?

Chapter Twelve

"The full hearing is going to be in two months," Yi retold Kwi Show. "There, they will decide whether I can have full custody of Shirley." She and Shirley were back living with Kwi Show. Even in the comfort of their home, they were not let to live peacefully. They frequently had visits from the Department of Social Services to check how the two were "getting along."

One day, a dietitian visited them to survey the eating habits of Shirley. Yi had prepared all kinds of food in front of Shirley, and hoped that Shirley would pick up something and eat. As if understanding the urgency of the matter, Shirley started to eat from her tray. The dietitian wrote down the report, and she was to send it to the judge.

Before the full hearing, Yi brought Shirley to see Dr. Robinson in January. Shirley was still on prednisone. Yi had called him during the case, and he had no way to help.

"I can clearly see that Shirley's condition is worse! If I had known they would treat you like that, I would never have recommended the doctor, Dr. Schelling, to you," remarked the doctor, a few frown lines appearing on his forehead.

"But I have never seen her. Shirley has always been seeing another doctor, Dr. Persse." Yi told him. She had always inquired about Dr. Schelling, but Dr. Persse, the one who had exclusively been seeing Shirley, only told her that Dr. Schelling would see Shirley later. But she never did.

"*What?* You have never seen the doctor I recommended?" The surprise scintillated in his eyes. He gaped; his mouth was wide enough to hold an apple. He fell silent. Yi did not understand this sudden change. Why the silence? She did not question him.

"I am taking Shirley to North Carolina," Yi told him.

After the appointment with Dr. Robinson, another appointment soon followed: Yi's next stop was at Boston's Floating Hospital for Children, as ordered by the court. The appointment was scheduled at two in the afternoon on February 5.

"It is snowing so heavily!" exclaimed Yi on the appointed day. "This is definitely not a good day." She had no other choice but to go. She wanted her custody—the right to be her daughter's own parent—back, so she had to bow to their demands. Agatha, too, was going. Samuel was to meet them at the hospital. Yi had not been sleeping well for a long time.

The tired Yi started the Cadillac, Dr. C.J. Ling's car. "There are already several inches of snow on the ground." She wanted to get it over with, quick.

The falling snow had made the visibility extremely low. Yi gritted her teeth. She could not believe what torment the hospital had put on them.

At long last, after over four hours on the road, the car stopped at the hospital, the inferno. Yi dragged her tired body out of the car while carrying Shirley out. Samuel greeted them by their car. "Thank you, Samuel!" She was so very much grateful for his support. "It is absolutely freezing," commented Yi. It was a freezing hell.

They went inside the building and reported their arrival to the receptionist.

Yi plopped herself in a chair in the waiting room, the rest followed suit. She carried Shirley on her lap. She hoped that the wait would be short, so that they could head back home before the snow got too deep. She looked around the room. She could not spot any patients.

One hour had passed without any murmur from the hospital.

Two hours passed. "When are we going to see the doctor?" thought Yi aloud.

When the clock showed that nearly three hours had passed, a woman appeared before them. "There are no doctors available."

"No doctors?" repeated Yi, frowning with puzzlement and annoyance. The woman shook her head and left.

The group looked at one another. "So, should we go?" pondered Yi. She was still hesitant to leave. She did not want to miss any doctors. She did not want them to find any fault with her.

After several minutes, she decided it was time to go. They had waited long enough. Yi thanked Samuel several times before they departed.

The sky was black as ink. Flitters of white forms swirled in the atmosphere. Yi turned the car around and turned onto the road of the ghostly ambiance. She had to drive very slowly in this chaotic weather. "The roads are extremely slippery!" exclaimed Yi.

Being four hours on the road did not even take them half way to home. "Slow" was not the word to describe the traffic. The snow was falling nonstop. All in all, it was an agonizing experience. Yi could hardly keep her eyes open. She glanced at the clock and saw that it was after midnight.

The time slowly ticked on. It was two in the morning and Yi's hands were stiff from driving. "They forced me to the edge of the cliff. If they treat real criminals like this, the world will be a much better place to live! This is the worst day to drive. The roads are so dangerous and we could get into an accident. And this is especially horrible when an extremely sick child is in the car. How could they do this to us? They know that we're coming," hissed Yi. She was fuming. She felt a sudden rush of warm current sweeping over her. She was infuriated by the torture.

"Looks like we're home!" declared Agatha half an hour later, peering out the window through the thick snow while stifling a yawn.

"Yes, finally! It is three already. It is absolutely outrageous," steamed Yi. "We went. They can't have anything bad to say about that."

***

The full hearing at last arrived, and Samuel had offered to go and represent her. "You don't have to be there; there is no need to," he said to Yi. He only needed to stay and listen to what they would decide. Yi waited anxiously at home for their decision. It seemed like she was waiting for the court to order a life sentence upon her; actually, it was much worse than a life sentence. Shirley's life was thousandfold more important than hers. How could she go on living without Shirley? And how could Shirley live without her? They needed each other like plants needed sunlight. Shirley's life was depending wholly on their decision.

Sitting by the telephone, Yi held Shirley close to her heart. She hummed a soft tune in Shirley's ears in the quiet room.

Ring!

Yi's heart gave a leap. The ring of the telephone invaded the silence like a bomb.

"You got the full custody back; the judge said! You are free!" Samuel reported on the other line. He had called Yi as soon as he returned to his place from the hearing.

Tears of joy ran down Yi's cheeks. She was speechless from being overwhelmed with happiness. She managed to thank him between her tears.

"I have helped you, and at the same time, I have helped myself. I told the case to my students. It is a good lesson for everyone to learn," he said. "And...I was fired by the hospital," he further told Yi. Both of them burst out laughing. The hospital had fired him after he helped Yi in her case. Yi was sorry about the unfortunate happening. She was surprised by such a low action of the hospital.

"Thank you so very much for all your help," she graciously thanked him again. She was immensely grateful for Samuel's help. He was such a nice person who would go out of his way to bestow kindness upon a mere stranger, expecting no rewards in return. Yi knew God was helping her during the case; He sent a kind man to be her interpreter.

She sat down on the couch and leaned back. She let out a long sigh. Ah, this was the taste of true happiness! Neither fame nor money could make her happier. She hugged Shirley tightly. The baby's small mouth stretched into a wide smile; she knew it was a happy moment for them both.

The telephone suddenly rang again. Wondering who it could be, Yi answered it. It was Melinda.

"Mrs. Cheng, you would still be under monitor," she told Yi. Monitored? What did that mean? But deep inside, she had a feeling what it meant. After hanging up with the social worker, she dialed Samuel's number.

"No, you will not be under monitor," he assured her.

Why did Melinda report falsely? But what did it matter? What did anything matter now that she had won? Yi's heart rested completely now. She and Shirley would live their lives again, with no more court sessions, hearings... Life would be grand once again. And her journey of seeking a treatment for Shirley would resume. The living nightmare had ended; they had awoken after a long, terrifying sleep of darkness. The music to the macabre dance had ceased.

Second Custody Case

Excerpted from Chapter Seventeen

On the twenty-fourth of May, Shirley made a hospital her home once again, and Juliet rented an apartment that was twenty minutes away. The hospital gave Shirley naproxen, but as before, it caused retrograde effects, including stomach ache. Meanwhile, she was also on the herbal medication, which was the only thing that was helping. The physical therapy was no better than naproxen. Shirley also received psychological evaluation during the stay.

The hospitalization did not provide any health benefits, and yet it did not worsen her health, either. It was apparent to everyone that the hospitalization was not improving Shirley's condition any. Dr. Zammit had suggested surgery for Shirley on six of her joints: both ankles, both knees, and both hips, all in a single operation.

"But Shirley's health is not yet stable. She cannot be operated on under such conditions," reasoned Juliet.

"Okay, so Shirley can leave the hospital; it's not helping her," he stated. After only three weeks in the hospital, Shirley was discharged on June 12. When would all this end? Would an answer ever be found? Or would they continue on this search that appeared to take them from one dead end to another?

Seeing that physical therapy was not the answer for Shirley, Juliet decided to take Shirley back to China for the fifth time. Juliet saw that the massages that Shirley received in China had worked well. She planned to stabilize Shirley's condition under the herbs and massage therapies. And if everything seemed stable, Shirley could probably get operated on her legs. It might work. Juliet, therefore, cancelled the lease to the apartment. She would move back with Kwi Show, and buy the ticket for August.

One peaceful day of glorious sunshine, as Juliet had her hands in soapy dish water, the telephone rang. She quickly rinsed the soap from her hands and scrambled over to the telephone. "Hello?"

"It's Dr. Zammit. I just wanted to check how things are with Shirley."

"I'm bringing Shirley back to China to do some massage." She had told him of her plans earlier.

"How about coming again for a checkup before you go? She can also see the eye doctor," he suggested. Juliet thought it was a fine idea and scheduled an appointment. It was scheduled for July 13 at 9:30 in the morning. Juliet checked the calendar, and saw it was on a Friday. She shrugged her shoulders. It was just another of those silly superstitions.

On that Friday morning, Ben rode with them when Juliet drove them off to Newington. Shirley watched the scene outside the windows, but it was hard to keep her photophobic eyes open. Juvenile rheumatoid arthritis could cause so many problems. One would think that the autoimmune disease was more than enough to endure, but the disease itself obviously did not think so.

Juliet carried Shirley into the stroller with the help of Ben. It was certainly nice to receive some help once in a while. Shirley shielded her eyes with the back of her hand. She took a good look at the building. She knew in a little while, they would be away from the hospital. She did not wish to stay in there again.

Shirley sensed something was amiss in the air as they were led to a room on the first floor by Dr. Zammit. She did not know what was wrong, but something was strange. Juliet could feel it as well. A smile was absent on Dr. Zammit's face, which was normally full of smiles. The room held many people who were dressed officially.

Time passed with none of the group of people moving. The sickening feeling increased in Juliet. The people looked at them attentively from their fixed places. What was going on?

Dr. Zammit reappeared before them, with a serious look on his face.

"Mrs. Cheng, do you want surgery for Shirley?" asked Dr. Zammit. Juliet answered him as the first time. Taking a look at Juliet with his unsmiling eyes, he walked away, while the crowd, as if on cue in a suspense movie, closed in on them.

"What is going on? What are you doing? Did I lose custody again, just like what happened the first time?" questioned the stunned Juliet. From the looks on their faces, her fear was confirmed. Juliet stood there, disbelieving the situation before her.

Shirley's heart pounded, but her strong eyes did not shed a single tear, nor did they blink.

A lady immediately pushed Shirley away from her mother to an adjoining room. Was Shirley afraid? Yes, but the feeling of anger invaded her being, flooding most of the space, leaving not much room for fright. What could she do? She could not speak English, only understand some. Even if she could speak, they were not here for reasoning. Their ears were not open to logic, nor their hearts to compassion and understanding.

Knowing the situation all too well, Shirley kept calm and composed. She colored in the coloring books the lady, whose position was unknown to her, provided. She knew if she broke down, it would make the situation worse. What the child did would be of importance on how they would judge the parent.

"I can't believe this! I made an appointment to see both Dr. Zammit and the eye doctor, but you just stop us from going back home. We came here freely. If we didn't come here, you wouldn't have come to our home and held Shirley. This is a dishonest action, and it is supported by so many people, not just an action done by one doctor," steamed Juliet. *What a bad example! Dr. Zammit had committed a crime, cheating his patient. Is there any difference between this and the capture of the Jews during World War II?* Her body trembled with shock and fury. How low could they stoop?

Juliet knew she could win this case, just as she was victorious in the first, for she had grounds. She had the reasons, and because of this, she could regain custody — the right to be the parent of her own daughter. What she hated and feared the most was the fact that this involved Shirley. If she were just fighting for herself, she would not worry — it would simply be fighting. What would she lose besides her life, which was so much less important than Shirley's? Now, since her daughter's life was on the line, it was so much more than just fighting; to her, the world was at stake. It was all about winning.

Shirley knew within her soul that her mother would defeat the battle between good and evil. She confidently looked at her mother as she was pushed away, down the hall and out of sight to the awaiting dungeon.

Chapter Eighteen

Juliet realized that it was a mistake to come to the appointment. She should have listened to the superstition. She was exhausted after talking for three hours with the social workers. She had wasted her breath talking to them. She might as well be conversing with stones from the apathetic reactions she received from them. They would not listen; they were here just doing their duties, separating families unreasonably.

As soon as Juliet got back to the apartment, she made several calls to her family, then to the local newspaper, the *Hartford Courant*. She told a journalist about her situation. After hanging up with the reporter, Juliet dialed the number to a legal aid service.

The next day, a journalist arrived at her apartment and wrote down all the information. After the young journalist left, Juliet drove to the lawyer's office to meet her new lawyer, Virginia. Virginia collected all the necessary documents and information for the case. With nothing else to supply the lawyer, Juliet left and headed to the hospital to see Shirley.

Juliet needed to feed Shirley the herbs daily, but she was only allowed to visit Shirley for ten minutes each day. It was not enough time to feed Shirley food and the herbs. She told the hospital this, but they were unrelenting; they did not even permit fifteen minutes. But at least she had the opportunity to administer the medication and give her cereal, which was the only food that could be eaten quicker than others.

One day, Juliet was giving Shirley Fruity Pebbles, but when it was time to drink down the milk in the bowl, Juliet needed to get a straw so that Shirley could drink the milk to swallow the herbal medicine without getting choked on the remaining cereal.

"No, Juliet, you don't have much time left," said the nurse who was monitoring them both as usual.

"But Shirley could choke on it," explained Juliet. No plea could give her permission to get a straw. Thus, Shirley had to drink the milk without a straw. Instantly, Shirley seriously choked on a piece of the cereal. It was a terrifying moment. Juliet watched helplessly as Shirley gasped for air. At last, her windpipe opened, and she was able to breathe. Juliet was furious at the hospital. They would not even give her an extra minute to get a straw for Shirley that could have prevented the accident from happening.

Shirley was often required to lie on her stomach upon a stretcher. They did not allow Shirley to sit up to take the herbs, so another serious choking incident occurred. The herbs, tiny small balls, were prone to cause choking if not taken in a proper position.

Juliet continued to make calls to seek help. One day, she received a call from a naturopath, Eileen. She had read the case in the newspaper, and had expressed an interest in helping.

"I can give Shirley some herbs, but not at this time when she's in the hospital. I will go there to see Shirley." And as she had said, she went to the hospital to visit Shirley the following week.

A few weeks into the hospital stay, the hospital had increased Juliet's ten-minute visitation time limit to two hours.

The landlord of the apartment had found new tenants, so Juliet had to move out and find another place that was close by the hospital. She moved into the Maple Motel that was three minutes away from the hospital.

***

Soon, Dr. Zammit put Shirley on methotrexate, an anti-cancer drug, saying it was beneficial for rheumatoid arthritis. As a result, Shirley quickly experienced extreme difficulty in breathing.

"You must stop the drug," demanded Juliet. "Shirley is having problems breathing!" But he would not cease the administration of the medication. Juliet sought Eileen for help at once.

"I'm subscribed to the *Cancer Control Journal*, and I'm going to read you the drug's side effects. It has a lot of adverse effects, but here are the main ones: upset stomach, nausea, vomiting, loss of appetite, diarrhea, mouth sores, headaches, dizziness, skin rashes, hair loss, coughing, fatigue, shortness of breath, lung damage, liver damage." Eileen paused for a few seconds to scan the journal. Then she continued, "The doctor on here says that sometimes an antidote doesn't work and the patient dies. The article also mentions that it is strong enough to kill the patient as well, along with the cancer."

"The drug's side effects are worse than the cancer itself!" exclaimed Juliet, listening on as Eileen read one horrid description after another.

Outraged, Juliet talked to Dr. Zammit again, and demanded that he stop giving the drug to Shirley. She waved the article in front of his face, while pointing at it. "Look at this!" She showed him the side effects where shortness of breath was mentioned.

"Well, I never knew that," he said. After persistent convincing by Juliet, Dr. Zammit finally gave in.

Shortly afterward, Juliet heard more terrifying news from the lips of Dr. Zammit. "We will do a general anesthesia test on Shirley,"

"Why? You are not performing the surgery for Shirley, so why does Shirley need the anesthesia test?" asked Juliet in bewilderment.

"We want to see how far her legs can be straightened. The physical therapist asked to do this."

"No," Juliet was defiant. But Dr. Zammit would not listen.

After she arrived home, she called up her lawyer. She had an idea that might just work.

"I would like you to help me do something. I would like you to come to the hospital to see Dr. Zammit. Please come to the hospital at one o'clock tomorrow. You tell him that Senator Dodd's office called you," Juliet told Virginia. "I can't have Shirley go through the unnecessary test." Dr. Zammit wanted to speak to Juliet that time, so she had asked for her lawyer to come then. It would be a nice scene. She inwardly smiled; he would not be braced for tomorrow.

Accordingly, right on time the next day, the lawyer went to the hospital to see Dr. Zammit. Juliet had arrived a few minutes earlier before her. A moment later, Dr. Zammit came into Shirley's room, where the two were waiting.

"I am from Connecticut legal aid service and Senator Dodd's office called me," the lawyer said to Dr. Zammit, as directed by Juliet.

"Oh," came from Dr. Zammit's lips.

Playing along, Juliet put a worried look upon her face. "Oh, she called me," said Juliet frantically, pointing at Virginia, "I don't know her! I don't want trouble! Why did she call me?" Juliet went on, pretending she did not know her own lawyer.

"Juliet said that you wanted to do the general anesthesia test on Shirley," continued Virginia.

"Yes," stated the doctor.

"You can't do it."

"We have to."

"Then if you want, go ahead. Have it your way..." The lawyer shrugged her shoulders nonchalantly. But by now, Dr. Zammit became less persistent. His eyes reflected doubt and hesitation. Juliet could see that he was falling for her trick.

"Okay, we won't do the test." He stated in the end. The parties split, with triumph in Juliet's heart. At least, she had successfully protected Shirley from this ordeal.

Within a two-week period after the nightmare had begun, Juliet attended the court session. Her lawyer was there, along with the social worker from the Department of Children and Youth Services. The intense moment would put much strain on any heart, making one cringe and run away. But Juliet stood tall and strong; her lips absent of any trace of a tremor.

Dr. Zammit went to the witness stand. "Shirley needs to have the surgery; it is best for her," he said. "The sooner she gets the surgery, the better it will be." There was no guarantee that Shirley would not be adversely affected by the operation. The surgery was not emergent, Juliet knew. It was not a life-threatening situation where Shirley had to have the surgery in order to live. The surgery could be done at a later time when she would be able to withstand both the surgery itself and the recovery that would follow. It was not just the surgery that she would have to endure; she would have to go through extensive rehabilitation and therapy afterward. Above all, how could Shirley have the surgery when the doctor did not even have any medicine to effectively control her current inflammation, not to mention the inevitable inflammation and complications that would follow the operation? This was not simply a life or death situation, Juliet knew; this was a paralyze or death situation, the ladder would be easiest on Shirley. She knew that without effective medicine to control Shirley's inflammation before and after the surgery, she would end up kissing her star goodbye or worse. So receiving the surgery at that time was unquestionably the worst option for her, not the best, as the doctor had claimed.

After Dr. Zammit finished stating his reasons, someone from the door announced Dr. Sheridan's arrival to speak for Juliet. Dr. Sheridan, a homeopathic physician, was found by Eileen, who was searching for a doctor to be on Juliet's side.

"No more witnesses," ordered the judge, not permitting Dr. Sheridan to come in.

Then the judge ordered immediate surgery for Shirley. "If the child dies as a result of the surgery, you cannot sue the doctor," she said, looking straight into Juliet's eyes, "you can sue me."

"Your Honor, may I speak for myself?" inquired Juliet after she saw that it was getting hopeless. No one was speaking for her; her lawyer was not helping any, either.

"You are not allowed. Juliet Cheng," boomed the judge, "you are a seven-year child abuser!"

When Juliet got out of the Hartford Juvenile Court, she spotted Dr. Sheridan, who was waiting for her. "I'm still here to help you," he assured her.

***

"The surgery will be next Tuesday," Dr. Zammit announced to Juliet a few days after the court session.

Her heart pounded wildly, but she did not show her panic. Her mind raced, thinking of another of her witty plans.

She immediately called up Dr. Simmonds. It had been a long time, she knew, but she hoped that the caring doctor might be able to lend a helping hand in this time of need. Was he still there? She fervently prayed that he would pick up the telephone. She glanced at the clock. It was late afternoon. "Please let him be there," Juliet whispered, her fingers quickly punching in the numbers. A woman answered the telephone. "May I speak to Dr. Simmonds?" asked Juliet. She was put on hold.

Soon, the voice that she was hoping to hear spoke into the receiver. Without losing a single second, Juliet began her tale.

"What is the name of this doctor?" asked Dr. Simmonds after Juliet had explained the whole story to him.

"Dr. Zammit."

"I know him. Well, you have the right to a second opinion. I know a pediatric rheumatologist in Philadelphia." Juliet was immensely grateful for his recommendation. "I will contact Dr. Zammit." Feeling much better after the conversation, Juliet finally could relax some.

Soon, she received a call from the Department of Children and Youth Services, telling her the appointment date with the pediatric rheumatologist in Philadelphia. It was scheduled in the noontime on August 30, a month later. Upon hearing this, Juliet was instantly relieved. She was so thankful for Dr. Simmonds' help. If without him, the surgery would go underway right away and Juliet would have no way of stopping it. Now, they had another month. She felt that whenever it seemed as though they had arrived at a dead end, a savior would come their way.

There would be a whole month without many bad things happening to Shirley. Shirley was already suffering enough in the hospital. She had blood tests done every week, usually on Tuesdays. But Shirley did not inform her mother of this, for fear of causing her worry over something about which she could do nothing.

By now, Juliet was allowed to visit Shirley for a whole day, but must leave before eight at night. She usually cooked some food at the apartment and brought it to the hospital. Each time, Juliet worked hard to get food into Shirley's mouth. But she was not allowed to feed Shirley, being accused of force-feeding, and the hospital monitored them whenever they got the chance. Whenever a nurse came in as Juliet was feeding Shirley, the nurse would immediately move her eyes to Shirley's mouth to see if Juliet was feeding her. When that happened, Shirley would stop moving her mouth or quickly swallow the food.

Juliet also bathed Shirley. When the hospital gave Shirley baths, she often caught colds, for they gave her only a few inches of water with mostly bubbles in the tub; the not-so-warm water quickly got cold. All in all, the days passed uncomfortably for Shirley. Her most pleasant moments were when Juliet visited her, often with a present. She had also given Shirley a few photographs of themselves, and Shirley held on to them when sleeping. Indeed, it was a sad time for the little girl. She had to bear the weight of those harsh times when she was so young. But Shirley kept on smiling, and found little delights whenever she could regardless. The wall above her bed began to be crowded by her drawings. Amongst them was a picture of a dinosaur she had drawn.

Juliet was surprised that she could draw so well and accurately, with quite a clarity.

Shirley never cried once in the hospital, not even when she was in pain. She enjoyed wheeling around the hospital, going past each room. She often sought other children to play with. But there was one particular girl who did not want to be with her. Shirley was quite puzzled at that, for Shirley had always been nice to her. But one day, when Shirley was dressed in a pretty dress that she had received as a present, the girl walked to her side and exclaimed with much astonishment, "You're a girl!" So that was it! The girl had thought Shirley was a boy, for her hair was short and she never wore dresses during hospitalization. Ever since that day, the girl gladly became her friend.

Besides roaming around and playing with others, Shirley received regular physical therapies at the swimming pool. Shirley liked the lady who was her regular therapist, for she was really nice to her. Shirley was able to walk while in the water. She often enjoyed the feeling of walking in the pool. But as Shirley was playing in the pool one day, her foot slipped and she went under. Reacting quickly, the therapist pulled her out of the surface. Shirley was gasping; it was such a close call. If she had been alone, she could have drowned. She became more careful while staying in the pool so not as to let the same thing happen again.

When Juliet came to visit Shirley, she often found Shirley waiting by the large door that separated one wing from another. But sometimes, the nurses closed the door when Shirley was waiting there. Thus, she could not have the view to the elevator, where her mother would appear. Often, when Juliet came, she brought a surprise or two for Shirley. One time, she bought a stuffed animal.

"Oh, a white dove!" exclaimed Shirley happily. She looked at the tag and learned that the name of it was Lovydovy. From then on, she had brought it wherever she went. On the few occasions when she did not bring it, people would ask where her Lovydovy was. One person had called it a duck. Shirley inwardly giggled at that.

Once, Juliet had bought Shirley two dozen balloons. When Dr. Zammit saw all the balloons, he bought Shirley one.

Sometimes, while visiting Shirley, Juliet had chances to talk to Dr. Zammit. "Why didn't you take away the custody the first time?" Juliet asked him, raising her brows.

"Well, I saw that your life was too hard then, so I didn't," he answered. "If Shirley gets the surgery today, you can bring her home tomorrow and you can go to China next week."

"Since you say that surgery is so good, what happened to those kids? Why don't you perform surgeries on all those kids upstairs? They are all like statues!" She had been upstairs and had seen many patients, whose every limb was immobile. They seemed to be blind as well, for their eyes never moved when Juliet walked to their side. Her heart went out to all of them. They had to suffer so much. Shirley was in a much better condition compared to them. She was able to sit and move her limbs.

Dr. Zammit never replied to that question. He had plausibly performed heaven knew how many surgeries on them! It was apparent that none of the treatments ever worked for them.

On another occasion, Dr. Zammit had brought a magazine for Juliet to see. "Look, can you see that surgery can be successful and that the patient can walk as a result?" he asked, pointing at a pair of photographs; one showed a disabled body, and the second showed a body that was walking.

"Where are the heads? How do I know they are the same person?" demanded Juliet. Dr. Zammit never had an answer to that question, either.

Chapter Nineteen

She was running toward a glistening stream with fish of all colors flying out of the water. With laughter escaping her lips, she chased a white butterfly amidst the green field of wildflowers. Her black hair glowed with a halo of brightness, with sunrays dancing about her. The blue sky was accentuated by a shimmering rainbow, which was surrounded by white, puffy clouds. Her mother watched her little girl, dressed in white silk, skipping before her. But her joy quickly turned into worry, for the girl was running farther and farther away toward the other side of the field until her little figure was no longer discernible.

"Shirley!" yelled her mother. The girl was disappearing from her sight. "Shirley!"

"What?" The groggy voice came from Shirley's lips. Her sleepy eyelids slowly fluttered open.

"Wake up, Shirley." A fuzzy image of a nurse came into Shirley's view, towering over her by the bed. The nurse went to the closet and picked out a pair of blue overalls. Shirley was enjoying the dream, but she was snatched back to reality. It was the day of the appointment, but it would not be for another hour till it would be time to go. She was awakened up just to dress? The nurse put the much too small overalls on her, practically stuffing her in like stuffing cotton in a small sack. Shirley could hardly sit up when she had the overalls on her. It was too tight. She felt cold and sleepy.

Before leaving her room, the nurse carried Shirley into her stroller. As Shirley thought of the appointment, Juliet walked in.

"Oh, why did they wake you up so early? It's only 5:15, and we won't need to leave till six o'clock!" Juliet touched Shirley's hands. "Dear, you are cold! Why did they give you such small clothes to wear?" Juliet went to the closet and picked something else.

"No, you can't change her clothes," ordered the nurse when she walked back in.

"I know what I'm doing; I'm her mother. We need to change them!" Without paying any attention to the protesting nurse, Juliet changed Shirley into a comfortable outfit. Shirley was feeling much better after the change, having more breathing space and feeling warmer. The nurse walked away, leaving the two alone in the room. The only thing left to do was to wait for the social worker from DCYS; they were to go together.

***

Mother and daughter boarded the plane, escorted by two social workers. Juliet had brought with them a few of Shirley's necessities. Soon, they would arrive in Philadelphia.

Shirley watched the scene from her window, while the two social workers talked with each other. Juliet meditated in her seat, hoping that the doctor they were going to see would help her.

They had transportation waiting for them as soon as they got off the plane an hour later. Juliet had carried Shirley on and off the plane, then into the car. They drove toward the hospital, Children's Seashore House (Children's Hospital of Philadelphia).

"I can't make the decision. The orthopedic surgeon needs to be here, so we can decide. You have to come here next time, and the orthopedic surgeon will be here," said Dr. Athorn after examining Shirley. Juliet felt comforted; at least he did not recommend surgery. The time was vital. Juliet must win as much time as she could.

***

"I know a lawyer who can help you." A man called Juliet one day to supply the information. "He was a former mayor of Hartford." After writing down the contact information, Juliet called the lawyer up. She got all the directions to his office.

That afternoon, she set out to meet her new lawyer George Athanson, who was the former mayor for eleven "and a half years," as he had insisted. Juliet felt hope surging in through her. She knew that this case could be won only by name and power, not by intelligence. Virginia had told her to find another lawyer, for she could not help her.

"I'm Romeo!" was the jocose greeting that came from George, as they met for the first time. They exchanged warm handshakes.

"Nice to meet you," said Juliet. She followed him into his office. It was cluttered with piles of papers. She gingerly made her way to a chair across his desk, which was nearly hidden under more piles.

"You are very busy," commented Juliet, her eyes taking in all the files, folders, and paper.

He nodded. "Yes, and I don't get much help and money, either. I need money, money, money!"

Very patiently, he listened as Juliet narrated the story. The conversation was filled with jokes mingled with serious talk.

"Why do you cut your hair so short?" he asked, raising a brow.

"It's easy to manage," answered Juliet with a laugh, absent-mindedly raking a hand through her black hair.

She handed him all the documents, but George had already saved all the newspaper clippings on her case. He handed her several business cards. "Tell them, 'This is my lawyer.'" He winked. Juliet accepted them graciously.

"I will pay you." After all was said, and several jokes told, they parted with another handshake. Feeling quite good inside, she got into her car. She knew for certain that she could win the case, and save Shirley from their grasp.

On the second day, Juliet gave George's business cards to the social workers, the doctor, and anyone else who was involved in the case. They read the name on the card with surprise and respect. She could see the immediate change they had with her now.

A week later, Juliet was scheduled for another court session in the Hartford Juvenile

Court. Before that day, George had told her that he met the judge the other day, and told the judge he had just accepted a new case that she was also involved in.

"Oh? Then which case is it?" the judge had asked.

"Cheng." Upon hearing this, the judge was startled and astonished. "How about a little help?" suggested George.

"No, absolutely not! Not with *this* one."

The day of the court session swiftly arrived, with Juliet bringing her new lawyer with her. All eyes turned in their direction, and they were surprised at the sight of Juliet with the former mayor.

"I have received the report from Dr. Athorn from Philadelphia. He recommended immediate surgery for Shirley," announced the judge. Juliet was immensely dismayed, but was not taken aback. She knew it was going to be this way. But still, she was not without hope.

The audience filed out of the court, including Eileen, who had taken her time to attend the session. She felt sorry that Juliet had to go through all this, and was disheartened by what the judge said.

"Shirley will have the surgery on Tuesday," Dr. Zammit told Juliet afterward.

It felt like deja vu. It was Friday, so she had to work fast. Frantically, she called George at his office at five. They scheduled to meet in a restaurant later that evening. At eight, he, with one of his assistants, met Juliet at a table.

"You must do something to stop the surgery!" Juliet threw a check on the table in front of him.

"I'll try my best." On Sunday, he called ten judges, but some were unavailable at the time.

Juliet anxiously waited at home. She could not let herself come to the realization that the surgery would be in only two days.

Chapter Twenty

What would happen tomorrow? It seemed that they had finally come to an impasse. Would they have a way out of it? The boat was filling with water, and sinking fast. If only they could have a way to patch up the large hole.

Shirley spent the day trying not to think about the next day. But no matter how hard she tried, her thoughts would always return to the surgery. She watched the clock tick on and on. Wheeling around the hospital, she passed a nurse. "I will have surgery tomorrow?" she managed to ask. She was picking up some English quickly, and was able to converse in English with extremely easy words.

"No, I don't think so," answered the nurse, and went away. Shirley hoped what the nurse said was true. Oh, how she had hoped with all her might!

"There must be a way, there must," Juliet was saying to herself at the motel. She would pay the lawyer everything she had, but all knew it would be fruitless. With her heart aching, she went to visit Shirley. Her face reflecting no worries, she came to see her beloved daughter, the one person who was so dear to her heart and soul. Shirley was the sunshine in her life. Shirley must live! She must be well!

"There will be surgery tomorrow, right?" asked Shirley, her eyes wide.

"No, there won't. We're trying." Juliet hoped she could keep her promise. She asked a nurse about the surgery when it was approaching six in the evening.

"I don't know anything about it," came the cursory answer from the nurse.

After hugging Shirley for a long time, not bearing to part, Juliet left with a heavy heart. She would go home and think some more. But before returning home, she drove to her lawyer's office. She had been calling him numerous times, but he would not answer the telephone.

"You must stop the surgery, you have to," pleaded Juliet once she got inside, towering over his desk.

"I just can't. I tried!" he barked. Without finishing to hear what he had to say, she drew more money out of her pocket.

"Here." She put down one thousand dollars. "Stop the surgery." He did not say anything else. His hands moved toward his head and he remained in this position. He could not stop the surgery even with all the money in the world. He was frustrated by it all. They needed to wait for a miracle to happen. Juliet was drained. She knew that George was, too. He had been working on her case exclusively, putting all other cases aside. He and his assistants often stayed up in the office late at night, putting their heads together to get Shirley out of the confines.

While the two were in the office, Shirley was on her hospital bed pondering about the surgery. It was the second time that she had heard of the surgery being on a Tuesday. She had prepared for the surgery last time, but to her unspeakable relief, it did not happen. She wondered if her luck would still be with her this time. The hour hand on the clock moved rapidly, making its way toward the ninth mark that evening. Shirley tried to go to sleep, but wanted to savor the moment. It might be her last night. She wanted the time to last long before tomorrow would arrive with its deadly deed. Dwelling upon the frightful event would not do her any good. She closed her eyes and thought of happy things as she drifted off to sleep, hugging the photographs and Lovydovy close to her heart.

Disheartened, Juliet left George's office and went home. Seeing that nothing was moving in the direction of victory for her, she sadly accepted the horrid fact. She had to know what time in the morning that they would perform the surgery for Shirley — the time they would plunge the chisel inside. She dialed up the number where she would be connected with Dr. Zammit, the man who had awfully wronged them. She left a message on the answering machine. She was fully prepared for the surgery. She sat by the telephone in full concentration. It was the biggest nightmare she had ever lived through.

Her heart gave a start when the telephone shrieked in the empty room. Dr. Zammit was on the other line.

"What time's the surgery?"

"There's no surgery," Dr. Zammit replied.

"No surgery?" Juliet repeated. Did she hear him correctly?

"Your lawyer cancelled the surgery. Didn't he tell you?"

"No." Juliet's soul lifted high until it touched the clouds. Her spirit was filled to the brink with exquisite elation, yet she did not let her voice show it. A mountain of fears and doubts had been taken off her shoulders. After hanging up, she called George. "The surgery is cancelled!" she happily announced into the mouthpiece. She could not stop laughing. It was the happiest moment of her life after a terrifying ordeal. They had escaped from a part of the nightmare. But she knew the nightmare had not ended, and it would be a while till it would. They still had a long, rugged road ahead of them.

"The surgery, *cancelled*? That's great!" He was taken by surprise. At least one of the judges he had called must have helped. They were so thankful for the decision. Shirley was saved once again! Juliet wished she could tell Shirley the wonderful news, so she could sleep in peace, but it was too late. With a triumphant and contented sigh escaping her smiling lips, she lay down on the bed. The past few days were a frightful experience that she would never forget. One man could bring forth such misery upon the whole family! But Juliet still did not have any hatred for him. She only felt sorry for him. He could choose to do so much good for his patients, but had blindly chosen this path. It had been some time since she had a good night's rest. Tonight, she knew, would be a fine one. She shut her eyes, her muscles relaxing. The September wind blew gently outside her windows. Trees whistled a tune of triumph and rejoicing. The caliginous sky held millions of twinkling eyes that winked to one another, knowing it was He who had helped.

Chapter Twenty-One

Early the next morning, Shirley was immensely delighted when she heard about the cancellation of the surgery. Her hope had helped. She looked in the mirror and smiled at her reflection. Yes, she was still here, alive and well.

But how much longer could they keep

this up? The surgery had been blocked twice, as well as a full-body anesthesia test. Juliet must win the custody case in order to save her pearl from a fate worse than death. There was no if's.

***

"I will bring the case to the federal court," stated George while Juliet was on one of her routine visits to his office. They needed to bring the case up to a higher level. It was not going anywhere at the Hartford Juvenile Court.

George leaned against his chair and shook his head. His eyes flashed with admiration when he commented on her invincible spirit. "You are just like Mao Zedong and Zhou Enlai. If you could, you would have fought with them for justice."

Once informed of the case, the federal court—the supreme court in Connecticut— asked for the court transcript from the juvenile court judge, but only received a rejection from the judge.

At the same time, a reporter from *The New York Times* called Juliet, asking if she could go to the hospital to take a few photographs of them. "It would be impossible for you to come to the hospital since you're from the newspaper," said Juliet. "But since you have the dog, you can bring it when you come to see Shirley. Just tell them you're bringing the dog for Shirley to see, and they would not expect you are from the newspaper."

The reporter arrived at the hospital dressed casually in a T-shirt, with her dog. As Juliet had predicted, she was able to visit Shirley in her room without raising any suspicion. Once inside, the reporter took out her camera and snapped shots of Juliet and Shirley. When she was done, she quickly left with a whole roll of shots.

"What's going on? What is this?" demanded a hospital staff member, showing an article to Juliet a couple of days later. It was the article and their photograph in *The New York Times* entitled *Can Choosing Form of Care Become Neglect?* by James Feron. Around then, an article of the case appeared on the *Newsweek* magazine entitled *Does Doctor Know Best? Overriding the Family* by Geoffrey Cowley with Lauren Picker.

"Go ask *yourself* what's going on!" Juliet fired back. Ever since that day, Shirley was not allowed to have any visitors to the hospital, except family members.

Meanwhile, upon reviewing the court documents (after a long while, the judge from the juvenile court finally relented and sent the transcript over), the supreme court decided to take up the case, which had not been fairly administered. The judge from the juvenile court had not allowed Dr. Sheridan, who was representing Juliet, to speak for her. It was only a one-sided trial of the hospital. It was an unjust case. Juliet knew that the juvenile court judge had made a big mistake in not letting Dr. Sheridan into the courtroom. The mistake became Juliet's victory, she knew from deep inside.

The supreme court then appointed a legal guardian for Shirley. Juliet won a reprieve when the supreme court judge ordered Juliet and DCYS to have an agreement: In a two-month period, Juliet was to find a doctor to treat Shirley, following the treatment of her choice; the doctor must be a licensed medical practitioner (M.D.), and the medical facility at which Shirley received treatment could be at any northeastern location, including Newington Children's Hospital. At the same time, Shirley's legal guardian should find two doctors: one an orthopedic surgeon, the other a pediatric rheumatologist. These three doctors in turn would determine whether Shirley needed the surgery. If two doctors stated that Shirley did not need surgery, there would not be any surgery for her. Otherwise, if two decided upon surgery, there would be one. After the two-month period, the court would arrive at a decision on the statements made by the three doctors. The term would end on December 10, 1990.

Juliet decided to have Shirley remain in the hospital to receive the treatment from Dr. Sheridan.

Therefore, Dr. Sheridan promptly put Shirley on his homeopathic medication, and all the other medications she was taking, including naproxen, the herb, and all laxatives, were dropped. The laxatives, glycerin suppositories and fiber tablets, had been administered to Shirley numerous times by the hospital because of her chronic constipation, but they had never been successful in relieving the condition, and instead had made her extremely uncomfortable. She normally ate small amounts of food, so each time after receiving the glycerin suppositories, the only thing that could come out was the suppository.

Dr. Zammit and the nurses said that Shirley's condition appeared to be worse. But Shirley was not well from the beginning, and it was too soon to judge the medication's effectiveness. Dr. Sheridan also let Shirley receive treatment from Regional physical Therapy in Hartford, so Juliet brought Shirley there three times a week.

Juliet continued to come to the hospital to bathe Shirley daily. Before, she was not allowed, but now the hospital had actually begun to depend upon Juliet for the bathing needs. Once, Juliet was too tired to bathe Shirley, for she had been traveling all day going to the lawyer's office and the court.

"No, you have to," ordered the nurse. Thus, Juliet had to bathe Shirley. Even though she was permitted to give Shirley baths, she was still not allowed to feed Shirley.

One evening, Shirley was running a fever, and wanted some ice cream. Juliet knew it was nearly time for her to leave, for the clock was ticking toward the eighth mark. She went to the hospital's freezer and brought over some ice cream. But Shirley needed help to eat it.

"Juliet, you have to leave. It's eight already," said a nurse, standing by the door.

"Wait, give me a minute, I only have half of this ice cream left to feed Shirley. Just give me another minute and I'll be done," said Juliet, holding out the half-empty four-ounce container of ice cream.

"No, you have to leave now. I will call the security man if you don't."

"Okay, you go ahead, go and call the security man." Juliet would not budge, and stood there vehemently, spooning the ice cream into Shirley's mouth. Shirley was quite frantic by now.

"Mom, you have to leave. The police will come." Juliet shook her head obstinately. She needed to tend to her own child. She would leave as soon as she finished feeding. There were only a few more spoonfuls to go.

Shortly, Shirley finished the ice cream. Meanwhile, the security man from the hospital, who, in fact, had been showing compassion for the two, had told Juliet to follow him downstairs. The nurse had just then threatened to call the police. Grateful for his offer, Juliet stayed behind him as they went down to the lobby. He escorted her to her car. Juliet hurriedly started the engine as police cars parked in front of the hospital. Breathing a sigh of relief, she drove away from the hospital grounds, safe and sound. All this had happened during a few minutes; the hospital clocks pointed to six minutes after eight.

***

One day, George received a call from CBS, asking if he and Juliet would go to their studio to be aired on *This Morning* show with host Paula Zahn, to which both consented. George and Juliet were picked up and drove to a large prodigious Hotel in New York City.

The next morning at eight, they were aired on the show. Paula started the five-minute live interview by asking, "Hi, Juliet, why do you not agree to have your daughter Shirley receive the surgery?"

"Because," started Juliet, "with rheumatoid arthritis, the inflammation is inside of the joints; the surgery will only fix the outside of the joints. If you don't have the powerful medication to control the inflammation inside, a successful surgery would still fail. The joints will go back to their original state, and would be even worse."

***

"CBS just called and said that one hundred doctors had called them, telling them that Juliet had well explained the reason for not wanting the surgery. And they wanted to help

115

Juliet in the case," a paralegal of George, had reported after they returned from the city. "They had never received so many calls after any show." The secretary of Taiwan's former first lady Soong May-ling was one of the callers who had expressed an interest in helping Juliet. Apart from the calls received at the television studio, Juliet had been receiving calls from various places and well-known people. Connie Chung left a message for her at her motel when she was out one time.

"Katharine Hepburn had written," Dr. Sheridan had told Juliet, "and she wishes to help you." Her case had been broadcast internationally, reaching China, Hong Kong, Canada, along with other countries. Once, Juliet had declined the invitation to New Jersey by NBC, for she had no time to go.

Meanwhile, under the treatment of Dr. Sheridan, the hospital still had blood tests done for Shirley weekly, as well as performing numerous x-rays on her. They knew that Shirley was staying there to receive treatment from Dr. Sheridan, and that they were not allowed to treat Shirley. Therefore, they were violating the agreement by doing blood tests and taking x-rays. Above all, drawing blood weekly was unnecessary.

One day, the nurse drew Shirley's blood without any success. After sticking the needle in Shirley's bony arm, not a single drop of blood could be drawn out. Taking the needle out, the nurse stuck it in again in a different spot, but with the same result. With a last try, the needle was stuck in a third spot. This time, only a tiny amount of blood was collected. Soon after, when the nurse left with Shirley's last drop of blood, dark blue spots began to appear on the arm, quickly spreading throughout her body. Shirley was frightened when she saw this happening.

When Juliet visited Shirley that day, Shirley was hiding herself under blankets and clothes.

"What's wrong?" inquired the concerned Juliet. Ever so slowly, Shirley took out her arm. "This is horrible!" Juliet was puzzled. *What could have caused this?*

"They have blood tests done on me every week. And today, the nurse couldn't get any blood out of me. Then this happened to me," explained Shirley in a low voice. Juliet was stunned. She had never imagined that this could have ever happened to Shirley. Why were they drawing so much blood from her so frequently? Were they vampires?

"Why didn't you tell me this earlier?"

"I'm scared. You can't help." Arguing with the hospital, they both knew, was useless. But Juliet silently vowed to herself that she would stop them from doing blood tests on Shirley whenever she could get the chance. No one had ever communicated to her regarding any tests, so she had to catch them red-handed. But whenever Juliet was with Shirley, no one would order any test or x-ray. Therefore, Juliet usually did not see them doing this until she had caught them in the act.

"No, you can't give blood tests for Shirley," demanded Juliet when Dr. Zammit called her one day after she had refused to let them draw blood from Shirley.

"But we have to do the blood tests for the doctors to see. They are coming..." he explained.

"No," she insisted.

"Okay, so we won't do it." Dr. Zammit gave in. "But we need to do an x-ray."

Juliet sighed, "Okay, go ahead." Therefore, an x-ray was done on Shirley's whole body.

Not only had Dr. Zammit ordered blood tests and x-rays for Shirley without Juliet's knowledge, but also had the hospital perform a tuberculin skin test on Shirley. The appalled Juliet steamed when she found out and told Dr. Sheridan, who expressed great dismay. But fortunately, Shirley's health did not worsen after the test.

Mother and daughter, hand in hand, still continued on their rough road, with each helping the other. Their strong bond of love had kept them going, never giving up for a minute. They were like a pair of binary stars, ever revolving around each other, and always emitting warmth. They would continue to strive to defeat the injustice. Justice shall always prevail in the battle against evil in the end. Inequity may use force and have weapons, but good has reasons and the powers of virtue.

***

"Why have you been scratching your elbows?" inquired Juliet after noticing that Shirley had been scratching her elbows and knees for a couple of days.

"I'm itchy," said Shirley, in a low voice. Juliet carefully examined Shirley's body and found bilateral, symmetrical rashes on both of her elbows and knees. If the rash appeared on her inner right arm, her inner left arm would bear the same rash.

"What could be the cause of this?" Juliet was growing quite concerned. The skin felt rough and scaly where the rashes were. Some rashes looked like burn-marks while the newer ones were small red bumps. She was perplexed.

The hospital applied some cream on the brownish rashes, but it did not help in curing the condition, only lessening the itchiness somewhat.

"You will have to go soon," noted Shirley, gazing at the clock. "It's almost nine." The hospital had extended Juliet's visitation time by an hour.

Juliet nodded and sighed. "Yes, it is time."

"Mom, I love you! I'll see you tomorrow."

"I love you, too, dear." Juliet gave a lingering wave. Then she went out the door.

Chapter Twenty-Two

On December 8, a pediatric rheumatologist, Dr. Thomas J. A. Lehman—Chief of the Division of Pediatric Rheumatology at the Hospital for Special Surgery in New York City and Professor of Clinical Pediatrics of Weill Medical College of Cornell University—went to check Shirley. He was one of the doctors the legal guardian had found.

"Would you like me to talk to you first or your mother first?" Dr. Lehman asked Shirley.

"My mom first," answered Shirley, smiling at the doctor, whose aura shone with nobility. His kind countenance tightly wrapped Shirley and Juliet in comfort.

Juliet followed Dr. Lehman out of the room and into the next, which was vacant.

"Why don't you want to do the surgery?" inquired Dr. Lehman.

"Because the doctor had told me that without surgery, Shirley would never be able to walk. But when Shirley was four and a half years old, she was able to walk for a year without surgery in China." Juliet took out the photographs, which depicted the event, and showed them to him.

"How beautiful that Shirley was able to walk!" he exclaimed, looking over each photograph.

"The medications that the doctors gave are not effective for the arthritis; they could not control the inflammation," Juliet continued, "They can't even control the inflammation, so how could they do the surgery? Surgery is just fixing the outside. We need to fix the inside while fixing the outside; not just fix the outside."

After the questioning and explaining were completed, Dr. Lehman examined Shirley.

Following Dr. Lehman, an orthopedic surgeon, Dr. Goldstein from the Boston New England Medical Center, was the next to examine Shirley on the tenth of the month. After completing, he left without directing a single question toward Juliet.

***

"Juliet, the reports are in," George told Juliet over the telephone four days later. The judgment day had at last arrived. Shirley's legal guardian had received all the doctors' reports, which held the key to either total destruction or the happiness that could only be elicited by the Garden of Eden.

Juliet headed toward George's office to wait for the sentence. Once there, she managed to pass all the reporters who were crowding outside the lawyer's office. She stepped into the tiny office, where George and two of his assistants, who were lawyers themselves, were found. Their faces exhibited high alertness. They each had the same thought: whether Juliet had won the case. Would Shirley be in Juliet's arms once again, or would she forever be out of the reach of her loving mother? They would exert so much force to break the steel bond of the inseparable pair.

Suddenly, the door to the office opened, and in walked a very tired legal guardian. "Gosh!" he exclaimed, shaking his head. He had a hard time getting away from the mob outside. The reporters nearly ran him down. He looked at the four people before him. They searched for an answer in his eyes, but could not read anything from them. They held their breath.

"Well," he said, clearing his throat to add to the suspense, "would you want to know the whole story or the bottom line?"

"The bottom line!" all cried in unison.

The legal guardian walked toward Juliet, put out his hand, and patted her right shoulder. "You won, you won, Juliet."

Juliet nodded, her lips spreading into the widest smile her face had ever owned. Was she surprised? No. She always had faith that she would win. Her confidence had grown more so during the past two months of the trial. She had been praying, seeking support and guidance from the Almighty One. Yes, He had answered her prayers.

"But even if you did not win the case," the legal guardian continued, "no surgeon from any of the hospitals throughout Hartford, including this one, is willing to do the surgery for Shirley." The internationally reported case had become the talk of everyone. The hospitals would not dare perform the surgery on Shirley even if Juliet lost the case. Juliet had many supporters, and it would have caused much trouble if they laid a single hand on Shirley when it was so strongly disagreed with.

One of the assistants, Steve, who always doubted her strong confidence of winning, went over to Juliet. "I believe you now," he said, shaking his head. Indeed, miracles do happen.

Juliet gave George a hug and a peck on the cheek.

"Hey, what about me?" asked Steve. Juliet gave him a hug and a peck, too.

Although the room was small, its happiness was radiating larger than the whole world. The celebration was not a loud one, but the expression on each face was more than any boisterous rejoicing could ever replace.

"So, do you have a back door?" inquired the legal guardian after handing George the three reports. Chuckling, George led him to the back door, where he could leave peacefully without getting trampled on by the reporters.

It was getting late, and Juliet was physically exhausted, yet her spirit had the energy she never before possessed; her soul floated on Cloud Nine. She could be with Shirley again! It had been five, long months. She had won the case, but only with His support, just as with the first. Before leaving the office, Juliet received copies of the reports from her lawyer. Closing the door, she thanked him once more.

The lobby was filled with reporters, each snapping shots around the place, while others held out microphones, hoping to catch something nice to air.

Into one microphone, Juliet simply said, "It's God's will."

Without waiting another minute, Juliet went straight to the hospital to give Shirley the grand news. On the road, she could not help but smile uncontrollably in her car. After she parked in front of the hospital building, she nearly jumped out of her car.

She flew into Shirley's room. "We won!" She did not need to say anything else, for those two words were clear in meaning.

Shirley was speechless from the elation. She joined her mother on Cloud Nine. The pair shared a huge embrace.

Suddenly, Shirley vomited on her pillow; she had vomited a large amount of blood. A nurse entered her room that moment and gasped loudly when she saw the blood.

Shirley was getting remarkably ill as days passed. They had been giving naproxen to Shirley on an empty stomach. They usually gave her only one spoonful of baby sauce with crushed medication. When Shirley asked for more baby sauce, they refused nearly every time. And thus, the burning sensation of the medication remained in her mouth, throat, and down to her stomach. At such times like this, she collected saliva in her mouth to wash it down.

Very soon, her stomach was bleeding, and vomiting began. Whenever Juliet had asked if Shirley had some food with the medication, they would only answer, "She had some JELL-O." Juliet had spoken to Dr. Zammit concerning the matter, and he had replied that he would speak to the nurses about it. And that was that.

Even though intense happiness filled Shirley, her illness would not permit her to celebrate it with much enthusiasm.

"You can bring her home now," a nurse informed Juliet from the doorway. The joyous news came as a surprise to Juliet. She did not expect that she could bring Shirley home so soon. It was already dark outside, but Shirley was excited at the thought of leaving the horrid place, even if it was midnight.

As Juliet was about to prepare for the return, Dr. Zammit walked in, a camera held in his hands. Shirley looked at him quizzically. A camera?

But before she could ascertain why he had brought it, the nurse turned to him and pointed at the bloody pillow. "Shirley just vomited." The doctor froze in his tracks.

Once he tore his gaze away from the pillow—and after the nurse left the room—he said with a smile, "I would like to take pictures of you." He held up his camera.

"But why?" asked Juliet.

"I want to remember you forever."

Is he crazy? thought Shirley. She shrank away when he got to her bed side.

"No, I don't want to take the picture," said Juliet, waving her hands, backing up. Dr. Zammit persisted, holding out the camera. Juliet waved her hands and shook her head again. She stepped back a few more paces.

"Well, can I take Shirley's?" He walked toward Shirley. Shirley wanted to scream no. She did not want him to take her photograph. Juliet reluctantly nodded her head. He snapped a shot of an unsmiling Shirley. With that, he walked off.

"He is so crazy!" commented Juliet.

"I didn't want him to take a picture of me," said Shirley, shaking her head with utmost distaste. He wanted to remember them forever? She knew with certainty that *she* would never forget him. She would never forget what misery he had brought upon them.

Dismissing the odd happening, Juliet began to prepare for the trip. She must work fast to get Shirley home before it got too late. Moving to the closet, she began to take out all Shirley's belongings. With as many bags as she could manage to find, Juliet stuffed all the clothes in until there was no room left for even an ant. She went in and out of the building to take the bags into her car, cramping them as best as she could.

Panting, Juliet dragged herself back into Shirley's room. It was, at last, time to bring her loved one home! She carried her daughter into the wheelchair. Shirley felt like a bag of bones in her arms. The child had suffered so much during the duration of the hospitalization. From being a girl with rosy cheeks and a healthy weight to sheer skin and bones.

With one last look at the hospital (and not a lingering one, either), they went inside the elevator that would take them away and close the door from the five months of living hell. Was this the feeling of the slaves after being manumitted?

Chapter Twenty-Three

It felt grand for both Juliet and Shirley to be finally together. Five horrid months had passed, separating them from each other. But the hospital had only managed to separate them physically, for they could and never would be spiritually separated. But the experience had left them with fear. Shirley knew that she would be fearful whenever she was to see a doctor. A third custody case could happen any time without any warning. How could she ever feel safe being with a doctor? They could do anything they wanted. Juliet could not speak out. She could not refuse any medical advice. Doctors, Juliet thought, should be friends of every patient. But how could they ever trust another doctor? Yet they had met some really wonderful doctors, such as Dr. Sabeston, Dr. Simmonds, and Dr. Robinson. They knew that they could not judge all doctors based on two negative incidents.

Shirley immediately felt her body recovering when they reached the rented house. Juliet had rented the house a month earlier, for she had planned to have Shirley start school when she got discharged from the hospital. It was December 14, and for the second time, it was right before Christmas Day. Was their reunion always going to be the present of the holiday season?

It was time to put the past behind them.

Juliet brought Shirley inside the house, their home for the time being. Seeing the cozy room, Shirley was rejuvenated.

"I would like to play on the floor," requested Shirley with glowing eyes. Juliet carried her onto the floor, and began to tidy up the place.

Ring! The telephone demanded attention. Juliet was hesitant to answer it, for fear of nagging reporters. But not wanting to miss any urgent calls, she decided to pick it up. Her suspicion was confirmed; it was a journalist. After hanging up, the telephone rang again. One call was followed by another; and all were from reporters from different newspapers and news channels. When the ringing telephone finally came to a stop, Juliet knew there were no more local newspapers left. But when Juliet was about to resume her cleanup, the doorbell rang. She knew all too well who was behind the door.

The reporters, along with their video cameras and notepads, swarmed in like hungry bees feasting on honey. She did not welcome them, but what choice did she have? Shirley was moving about on the floor as they took shots of her. She shyly smiled into all the hungry cameras. They asked her how it felt to be home, and she replied that it was good, wishing that she knew better words to describe how she really felt. Juliet did not know who was who, but she knew the *Hartford Courant* and The Associated Press were there.

"Your news will be aired tonight at eleven," said a man with a video camera hoisted upon his shoulder. Shirley was excited. She wished to see the news, but she was quite sleepy and could not stay up that long.

Juliet breathed a sigh of relief when the reporters left, satisfied with the information they had gathered. Juliet tucked Shirley into bed, and continued with her work.

Once snuggled under her cover, Shirley's eyes soon closed; she would surely have a fine night for the first time in a long while. She could sleep in peace, and would not wake up to the dreary life of the hospital.

In the living room, Juliet finally got everything tidy. She plopped on a chair before the television. It had been an exhausting time for her, but it was all worth her effort; she had won the case, and that was the biggest reward that any mother could ask for. "This case is ridiculous. It was beyond belief," she said to herself, repeating what she had been telling reporters. She thought about the news articles and shook her head. No article mentioned the fact that Shirley had actually walked for a whole year in China and that she was cured using Western medicine, not Eastern. She had given a photograph to *Hartford Courant* that showed Shirley walking, but the newspaper had printed the photograph with only Shirley's head showing.

The clock was ticking toward eleven, so Juliet turned the television on, and waited for the news to begin. "Oh!" A small cry escaped her lips when she saw her daughter on the set. Shirley looked beautiful with large, smiling eyes and shining shoulder-length black hair. Juliet did not catch much of what was said, for she was captivated by the images.

Afterward, Juliet got out the doctors' reports and scanned through them. She saw that each doctor, including Dr. Goldstein, had made fine points. But why did Dr. Goldstein recommended immediate surgery when the statements in his report clearly indicated that the surgery would be highly risky in Shirley's current circumstances? From the reports, Juliet also arrived at the conclusion that the psychologists had made false accusations about

Shirley's personality and behavior. She felt more stunned than anguish at first, but the feeling slowly turned to anger. Shirley was never once depressed during the duration of the custody case, though she was naturally apprehensive for her future health status. Would anyone not exhibit the same feeling if they were in her situation? But she was not the least bit apprehensive when Dr. Goldstein examined her, unlike what his report implied.

The readers could now take part in examining a few excerpts from the three doctors' reports below:

Dr. Sheridan
December 6, 1990

"...Shirley came to the hospital in a very frightened state (this last according to the nursing staff). When I met Shirley, however, she was alert, bright, and not at all frightened or shy."

"There has been a great concern expressed by all parties (Mrs. Cheng, the staff at Newington Children's Hospital, and myself) regarding Shirley's eating habits."

"In working with the nursing staff and with Mrs. Cheng in the last two months, I believe that more time was spent on this than any one other issue in Shirley's case. It became apparent to me that the fundamental issue could be Shirley's loss of appetite (rather than the mother's force-feeding), and that if the appetite could be corrected all the behavioral issues could be resolved."

"In addition, should surgery be forced upon Shirley, without her mother's consent, I believe that the involved stress would severely compromise any good that the surgery might do."

Dr. Lehman
December 8, 1990

"Psychological evaluation has shown that Shirley has several deficits and indeed psychology shows that she is depressed and exhibits marked oppositional behaviors throughout her hospital stay.

"On examination by me today, Shirley is an awake, alert, oriented, but anxious and somewhat tearful Chinese female in no acute distress."

"In regard to the specific questions asked today, I do not feel that emergent or immediate surgery is necessary for Shirley's ultimate benefit. The complexity of her illness, the poor yield in long-term management with surgical releases and the confounding factor of both Shirley's mother and Shirley's personal disbelief in American medicine and the benefits of the procedures to Shirley, mean that her recovery will be marred by poor effort and perhaps even overt opposition on the part of both Shirley and her mother. This opposition is likely to outweigh all potential benefits of the surgery since the recovery from the surgery will be marred substantially if there is not intensive effort to overcome the associated pain at the time of physical and occupational therapy. Shirley's ultimate well-being requires that she not only undergo appropriate medical care from a strictly scientific point of view but in order to recover from the pain with the procedure and do well, she must have a significant level of belief in the benefits of the therapy and significant effort must be invested on her part to recover appropriately."

"Absent the belief and willingness to invest significant effort to overcome pain and limitation secondary to surgical procedures, such a procedure has low potential yield for recovery of true ambulation."

Dr. Goldstein
December 10, 1990

"A detailed psychological evaluation revealed an eating disorder, a dependant personality, and comprehensive skill deficits."

"She is a thin female with a chronic illness, friendly, but somewhat apprehensive."

"If the goal is walking, it is my opinion that medication, and physical therapy modalities will not be sufficient, an orthopedic surgery will be needed. If one looks at only the bones and joints, it is apparent from her x-rays and from the contracture on physical examinations, that there are clear and straight forward indications for surgery on both feet, both knees, and both hips. However, if we look at this child there are other issues that might override or even preclude a decision to operate. This includes family investment in the process, the cultural and psychological factors, the risks of complications, the risks of reoccurrence, and the natural history of JRA. If one is to measure the "episode of illness" and therefore the duration of treatment, it goes well beyond act of surgery. Without commitment, without assurance of long term compliance, the likelihood of surgical failure and of reoccurring deformity is great."

Third Fright

Excerpted from
Chapter Sixty-Three

Shirley requested to go to the emergency room again the following dawn. "I'll call an ambulance for you this time, okay?" It was hard on both of them when Juliet had to carry Shirley in and out of her car. Shirley nodded in agreement. It was five when Juliet dialed for an ambulance. "My daughter can't breathe and she needs to go to the hospital."

Soon, the ambulance arrived. The paramedics rushed into the room.

"Is she conscious?" asked one paramedic.

"Yes, she just can't breathe well."

"We're going to give her IV."

"No, there's no need for it."

"You are uncooperative."

"Just don't do it," insisted Juliet. She had enough experience with the medical system already. She knew too well that no matter what caused the emergency, the paramedics would automatically stick a needle in the patient's arm. The unhappy paramedics relented to Juliet's order.

They carried Shirley onto the stretcher and lifted her into the ambulance. It was the first time that she had ever been in one. She weakly looked at her surroundings, but quickly closed her eyes. The energy needed to move her eyes was leaving her no more energy to keep them open. The shallow breathing and tightening of her chest had enervated her soul, leaving barely enough energy to lift a finger.

Juliet followed the ambulance close behind as it rushed to Vassar Brothers Medical Center. On the road, the paramedics checked Shirley's blood pressure and pulse. They put an oxygen mask on Shirley's face. They did not turn on the siren, for which Shirley was glad. She would be unable to stand the loud sound. She needed as little noise and disturbance as possible.

They lifted Shirley out of the ambulance and into the emergency room. She squeezed her eyes when the lights invaded her field of view.

The hospital staff came to tend to Shirley without having her to wait. Coming in from an ambulance was much faster and received more promptness than coming in by other means.

Shirley continued on the oxygen for a while, then they switched her on a nebulizer machine. There was no information passed between the hospital and the patient. During all the years of Shirley's hospitalization and doctor visits in America, the hospital seldom shared with her information concerning her examination readings. Everything was kept as a secret. Thus, her oxygen count was not told to her, either. But she knew it was low from the looks on their faces.

The nebulizer machine provided slim help; Shirley's chest was still tight.

"She can go home now," announced the doctor. They had nothing else that could ease Shirley's suffering. Juliet was numb from the whole ordeal. She would find another route after bringing Shirley home.

Juliet noticed that the staff had just changed shifts. A new doctor traded places with the doctor who had attended to Shirley earlier.

"Who is her pediatrician?" asked the doctor on the new shift.

"Dr. Madison," replied Juliet.

"Let me make a call." With that, he turned and left.

Juliet sat back down in the chair by Shirley's bed. Shirley wanted to go home right then. She needed to lie down and go to sleep. She did not sleep well at all last night.

Moments later, another doctor appeared. To her dismay, Juliet saw that he was the same doctor to whom she had first suggested that Shirley had pneumonia.

"She needs to be admitted to the hospital," he said.

"No, I need to take her home. She can't stay here," answered Juliet, firmly.

"If you don't have her stay in the hospital, I'll call the Child Protective Services," he threatened. "She's too sick to go home."

"You go ahead! Call them! Call them!" Juliet was furious. She had enough of it all.

Every time they had treated them as puppets on strings, and if they would not listen to their preemptory command, Child Protective Services would be called in. Juliet knew that Shirley was extremely sick, but she also knew that the hospital would not be able to offer any help. At home, she could think of some way.

"Mom, don't say that! What if you'll lose custody again?" said Shirley in a low voice.

"Don't worry. They can't do that to us." But they both knew that they could do anything to them.

More energy was drained from Shirley as a result of the fright. She would not be able to stand another custody case! She just could not!

"Don't worry," repeated Juliet.

Shirley's keen ears quickly caught the sound of a set of distinguished footsteps. A smartly dressed woman came into view and walked over to them.

"Hi, I'm Mary, and I'm a social worker from the hospital," she introduced herself, handing Juliet a business card.

Shirley forgot she even had a breathing problem. All her thoughts turned to the woman before her, waiting for the life sentence.

Mary took a chair and sat down facing Juliet, who began to tell her the situation. Mary listened patiently with nods between Juliet's words.

"You can take her home," said Mary when Juliet finished.

"What?" asked Juliet in disbelief. "I can take her home?"

"Yes."

"I can't believe it!" *Even at such a life and death situation, I can still take her home*, thought Juliet. *Why did they not allow us to leave in Newington? We were just going there to see the doctor, just like this time except that this is an emergency visit rather than an outpatient one.* It truly flummoxed her.

Then Juliet explained her reason for wanting to take Shirley home. "Shirley has been here for two hours and I didn't see any improvement. If I take her home, I may have slight hope to have different treatment for her. In here, Shirley will be disturbed. They will do unnecessary testings for her. I can't tend to her. She can't eat or drink whenever she likes. Everything will be hard to do. If she's at home, I can get her to sleep, give her a sip of a drink… I can really take care of her at home." She clearly knew that if Shirley died when she took her home, she would be charged with murder. But for the tremendous love for her daughter, she would risk it.

"Yes, that's true," agreed Mary, nodding her head. "I see your reason. You can take her home now."

"Thank you so much! Shirley will have a much better chance of living. Thank you!" Mary shook Juliet's hand before leaving.

"Thank goodness for her," said Juliet, immediately carrying Shirley into the stroller.

Shirley was extremely nauseated at the time and felt highly uncomfortable, but she had managed to smile and look well at Mary's presence. She felt like vomiting any moment. She was trying her hardest not to do so. She needed to get back home as soon as possible, so she could vomit. She had never felt as ill as she was now.

On the road, Shirley vomited all over herself. "I had been holding it in all this time," said Shirley.

"Poor dear. I'll get you home soon."

"I feel a bit better after I vomited." Shirley did not look down at herself, fearing that it would nauseate her further. She was certain that it was all mucus just as previous times. Her lungs were filled with sputum. She wanted to get all of it out of her lungs.

Chapter Sixty-Four

Juliet massaged Shirley's head as she slept. Shirley's breathing was rapid and shallow. Whenever she had pneumonia, she did not snore. A plumber was working in the adjoining bathroom of the master bedroom. Juliet had scheduled this appointment a long time ago. He was to take away the toilet and construct a shower place for Shirley. But today, he would not start on the construction, for it would make a lot of noise. It was pivotal not to disturb and wake her up. Thus, he only could take away the toilet. After his work was done, he quietly left the condo as instructed by Juliet, who had informed him of the situation.

Juliet knew that Shirley would continue to live. She could not bear it if Shirley left the world. She would miss her so much. She was her entire life—she depended upon her entirely.

After some time had passed, Juliet quietly got up from the bed. Shirley was such a light sleeper; the tiniest sound could wake her up. There was still so much left to do for Juliet. All the visits to the emergency room had resulted in everything else unattended.

Her movements were quiet, and yet quick, as she moved about in the rooms. Still, the floors cracked under her feet. *It is not a very good construction*, thought Juliet. She had wanted to move to another complex, one that was much better, but the school district was not as good, so she chose this place over the other one. Then she thought there was another reason of picking this place over the other one: the driveway access was poor unlike the condo, where it was convenient; Juliet could park her car right in front of the condo.

She sighed when her thoughts turned back to Shirley. When would pneumonia invade her body again? "Is it going to turn into pneumonia whenever she catches a cold?" Juliet asked herself. It appeared to be so. And what was most frightening, more frightful than pneumonia itself, was asthma. She was stunned when she had learned that Shirley had asthma. It seemed as if it would be stuck with her for the rest of her life. It was the most frightening disease that Shirley had encountered so far. She knew that asthma was serious — she had heard awful stories of it.

Then, she thought she heard Shirley calling her. She quickly stopped what she was doing and went into the bedroom.

"Pearl, did you call me?" asked Juliet.

Shirley had her eyes opened somewhat and was looking at somewhere unknown. "No, but I was just about to call you."

"Then, I just came right on time!" Juliet smiled. It was not rare for such an occurrence. Sometimes, Juliet would think she had heard Shirley calling her, and she would come to find that Shirley was just thinking of calling her. It seemed as though they sometimes communicated through telepathy.

"What do you need? How do you feel now? Better?"

"I do feel a little better." She took a deep breath. "My chest doesn't feel as tight. I would like to sit in the living room."

"I'm so happy to hear that!" She was so much relieved. It had been so close. "Sure, let me get your wheelchair." After getting the wheelchair beside the bed, Juliet carried Shirley onto it. She pushed her down the short hallway and into the living room. Shirley had not gotten a chance of a good look at the place.

But they did not have the quiet moment to themselves for long, for the door sounded with a few quick knocks. "Who could that be?" pondered Juliet out loud, rising from the couch. Deep inside, she had a sinking feeling who could be behind the door.

"Is this Juliet Cheng?" asked the woman. From her official outfit, Shirley knew it was not a visit of which they would be glad.

"Yes."

"I'm from Child Protective Services. I am just checking on how things are."

"Oh, please come in." Juliet stepped back, opened the door wide, and invited her in.

After they seated at the sofa and Shirley situated herself in front of them, Juliet started telling her the situation. The woman listened without interrupting. "She is better now after a nap," finished Juliet. Shirley gave her a wide smile as a confirmation.

"Yes, she does look nice," the social worker smiled back. "Well, that's all I wanted to know. Glad she's doing better. I'll check on her later." She stood up, bade a temporary goodbye to the two, and went out the door Juliet held open for her.

Two simultaneous sighs were released following the closing of the door.

"She startled me," said Shirley.

"Don't worry. I was expecting such a visit," stated Juliet, shaking her head. "At least, they are nice people. We are fortunate this time." Shirley nodded in agreement. "Or else, they would give us trouble." Shirley nodded again.

***

"Mom, I need to go to the hospital again," announced Shirley.

Juliet gasped. "But not back there again," she said, referring to Vassar Brothers Medical Center. "Oh, but where can I take you?" thought Juliet, frantically. *There are only two hospitals in this whole area,* thought Juliet. *Where can I take her?*

Then and there, Juliet knelt by the foot of the bed and prayed to God, asking for a place to take Shirley, who was starting to gasp for breath.

Suddenly, a name formed in Juliet's mind.

"Medicus!" She felt a surge of abundant energy sweeping over her entire being like a lightning bolt.

"Medicus? What is that?" asked the puzzled Shirley.

"It's like an emergency room. But I am not sure how to get there. I think there is one by your grandmother's house, but I don't know the directions!" Quickly, Juliet thought of the realtor, who had helped her in buying the condo and dialed up her number.

"Hi, Lauren? Yes, it's Juliet. Fine, thank you. Yes. Oh, it has been terrible. My daughter is really sick. Do you know how to get to Medicus? Oh, really? There's one here close by? That's wonderful! How do I get there?" Juliet listened anxiously as the realtor told her the directions. "Thank you so very much! Yes, I'll take her there now." She quickly hung up and glanced at the clock. "I hope it's not too late. I need to give them a call. I hope they don't close too early on Saturdays!" It was well past five in the afternoon on the same day they escaped Vassar Brothers Medical Center. She needed to act fast. She called information and obtained the number to Medicus. She called them up.

"What time do you close today? At eight? Okay, thank you."

Juliet knew she needed physical strength to go through the trial that lay ahead. She quickly wolfed down a slice of wheat bread which Shirley liked and she despised. Then she took some vitamins, and off they went.

It was six when they got on the road. Juliet glanced at Shirley beside her several times on the road, clearly seeing that she was suffering on a grand scale. It had been worse than before. Shirley's lips were turning blue and her eyes glassy. She prayed that Medicus would be the holder of good news.

"Here we are," announced Juliet, parking in front of the primary health-care center. "There are only a few cars here. Good — it will be faster."

Juliet pushed Shirley to the door and opened it, noticing it was quite heavy, but it would not remain open. It quickly swung shut. Someone then came to their assistance. "I'll hold it for you," offered a kind, elderly woman.

"Oh, thank you so much!" Shirley whispered her thanks as well.

"My daughter is here to see the doctor. She can't breathe."

"It's an asthma attack!" exclaimed a nurse as soon as she saw Shirley. They asked for her to be pushed into an examining room immediately. Juliet turned her around, so that it was a better position for examination.

Shirley looked like a gasping waxed doll, sitting limply in the stroller. The nurse held out a machine to Shirley and asked her to put it in her mouth. "Blow into the mouthpiece," she instructed. Shirley blew as hard as she could, but she merely forced out a tiny amount of air just enough to blow a feather from a table.

The doctor came in then and quickly went to work on her case. Together, the two brought over a machine and gently inserted the mouthpiece into Shirley's mouth. Shirley took quick breaths.

As if by magic, Shirley felt her chest loosening by the second. And after merely a minute's use of the wondrous machine, she could breathe freely on her own.

"Look, she can breathe, and she looks better now!" exclaimed Juliet, completely taken aback from the miraculous happening.

"Yes, she looks *much* better," agreed the nurse, her lips curling into a big smile.

"I feel so much better now. I can breathe again!" said Shirley, a happy smile touching her lips, which were regaining their color. Shirley had never before recovered so swiftly and so completely. She felt like a whole new person.

"It's amazing! How were you able to do it?" inquired Juliet, amazement engulfed her voice.

"We use oxygen combined with the medication. This way, it will open the lungs, so the medicine can get into the lungs fast, unlike the usual way that other people do it — that will not open the lungs and therefore, the medication could not get into the lungs," explained the nurse, supported by the doctor, who repeated the same words.

"This is a miracle!" exclaimed Juliet. "This is wonderful." She laughed, joy radiating throughout her entire being. "Why don't others do the same thing?"

The doctor and nurse shrugged. Everyone should know such a golden secret to treat the horrid condition!

The joy-filled pair left only after thanking the two saviors profusely. Medicus had saved Shirley's life. Juliet would never forget them. She felt at ease at last as she drove home.

Chapter Sixty-Five

Shirley speeded around the new condo in her power wheelchair that they had custom-made for her a few months before. She went in and out all the rooms, curved around the halls, and entered the living room where she had started, all done with a wide smile.

"It is very nice here," Shirley chirped. "More space and room here."

Shirley even had an office of her own in the second bedroom. It had all her school materials, along with her desk with the computer and printer, on it. A bookshelf full of books was situated to the right. The condo was not a big place, but it was enough for the two of them. And it was quite convenient with two bathrooms, one of which was in the master bedroom. Juliet had the toilet there taken out and the construction of a shower place for Shirley was going underway.

But nothing could ever be perfect: the condo had one faulty feature. At the doorway, where it led to the parking lot, there was a step that was a few inches higher than the ground, thus it would be hard for Shirley to go in and out of the building. Shirley's power wheelchair was powerful, but the sudden jerks resulted from going down the step hurt her joints. Juliet had to think of a way to level it.

It was the first time Shirley had an opportunity to see their new home. She was still weak from the illness, but after a couple of days had passed from the visit to Medicus, recovery began. "It is nice here," repeated Shirley, trying to get Juliet's attention, who was mulling over something.

Juliet had been calling Medicus to ask about their secret remedy since a couple of days ago, but only received angry replies in return. What was even more disturbing was the fact that the two people who had saved Shirley denied ever saying about the "oxygen combination" to "open the lungs."

"You kept calling and calling here! We never said that. I have no idea what you are talking about," the doctor had said, his voice rising.

Juliet was stunned. It seemed as though the doctor and nurse had been abducted by aliens and then brainwashed.

Juliet dialed the telephone again and asked to speak to the doctor.

"Sorry, ma'am, but he doesn't work here anymore," said the receptionist.

Numbly, Juliet hung up. So, with their secrets, they had vanished into thin air. At least, Shirley had been saved and that they had learned the magic cure. From now on, she knew what to request from doctors.

"They said that they never said anything like that, about combining oxygen with the medication," said Juliet.

"That's so strange."

"Yes, I know I wasn't imagining it—you heard it, too."

"Yes, I did."

"How do you feel now?"

"My chest is much better, but sometimes I have a hard time getting a deep breath."

Shirley's eyes wandered to the sliding doors. "It's a nice day out," she noticed.

"Would you like to go for a stroll?" Shirley nodded. "It's not windy out today. I'll bring your jacket just in case." Seeing that all was set, she opened the door and together, they went out.

They nearly bumped into a woman who was just coming in the main entrance of the building. Mother and daughter simultaneously recognized the woman. She was the social worker from Child Protective Services who had been there not long ago. Juliet promptly led her in, with Shirley following behind.

Like the first visit, the second was short. The social worker was simply checking to see how Shirley was doing. Shirley hoped it was the last visit from any social workers as the woman stepped out.

Give Parents the Right to Say No Petition

On the great Martin Luther King Jr.'s Day, January 15, 2007, Shirley Cheng created the Parental Rights in Children's Medical Care: Give Parents the Right to Say No Petition to return rights to the hands of loving parents. Mr. King opened the eyes and hearts of people to accept fellow mankind, now it is Shirley's turn to open the eyes and hearts of people to protect today's parents and the children of our future.

Please sign the petition to support a great cause at: www.petitiononline.com/parentr7/petition.html

Should the state send parents to court just because the parent told the hospital that aspirin is worsening their child's condition? Is it okay for the judge to call the parent a child abuser when the parent intercepted unwanted, harmful treatment for their child?

If you want to stop this power abuse, injustice, from striking another innocent parent, then sign this petition. The next victim may be your grand child or your best friend's daughter or the woman next door.

What the Public Thinks...

I am conducting two one-question polls on my website to allow the public to vote anonymously. The polls are ongoing indefinitely, so you are welcome to cast your own opinion.

The first poll asks: Who should make the final decision in children's medical care?
As of January 2008, there are thirty-five votes, and the results are:
The doctor......1 vote......2%
The parent......25 votes......71%
The child who is old enough to understand......9 votes......25%
Vote: www.opinionpower.com/Surveys/354037681.html

The second poll wants to know: Should parents have the right to disagree with doctors' recommended treatments for their children?
As of January 2008, there are fifty-three votes, and the results are:
Yes, parents should......49 votes......92%
No, parents should not......4 votes......7%
Vote: www.opinionpower.com/Surveys/123037682.html

About the Author

Shirley Cheng, born in 1983, a blind and physically disabled award-winning author (with twenty book awards), motivational speaker, self-empowerment expert, poet, author of seven books and contributor to ten, is a miracle survivor with tremendous talents, an exceptionally tenacious spirit, and a colorful personality. She was diagnosed with severe juvenile rheumatoid arthritis at only eleven months old. She spent her early years in constant pain, confined to a wheelchair, and was hospitalized for many years while living between China and America until 1994. Unable to receive any form of education until her health was stabilized, Shirley started attending school at age eleven in a special education class in elementary school. Back then, she knew very little English, and her knowledge on other subjects was non-existent. Miraculously, she mastered grade level in all areas after approximately 180 days of attendance, and she immediately entered a regular sixth grade class in middle school.

Shirley has a voracious appetite for books, reading an average of six hundred pages (three books) daily, and has read over a total of two thousand books. Since sixth grade, she has received 100 on every NYS essay test, and stayed at the top of the class ever since. She was awarded for achieving the highest grade of

97 in Earth science in her eighth grade class. She was the Student of the Year and the Student of the Month, as well as a three-time winner of the National Reflections Program in visual arts. She has a passion for writing both prose and poetry. Two of her writings were published when she was fourteen and fifteen. One of her short stories, *Mary Miller, the Elusive Lady*, received Honorable Mention and was published by the *Poughkeepsie Journal* in 1997, and her poem, *The Colors of the Rainbow*, earned merit status and was published in *Celebrate! New York Young Poets Speak Out* in 1999.

Shirley was a contributor to her high school newspaper, providing artwork in tenth grade. She received a standing ovation when she delivered a speech as a candidate for student body vice president in ninth grade.

When her eyesight began to deteriorate at the beginning of tenth grade, she had to use two magnifying glasses, holding one on top of the other, on enlarged print to do her work throughout the year, including the artwork she provided for the school newspaper. In classes, she learned only by listening to her teachers, even with chemistry and math, as she was unable to see the blackboard; still she maintained excellent grades.

Unfortunately, Shirley completely lost her vision in April of tenth grade. She then received home-tutoring, and successfully completed all her schoolwork by using cassette tapes and tape recorders. She wrote and balanced long chemistry formulas and equations without vision or Braille (she cannot use Braille because of her severe arthritis). Her high school overall average was 97 (a 3.9 GPA without any advanced placement classes). But Shirley could not accumulate enough credits to receive a high school diploma from her school due to her vision loss. In 2002, she received her high school equivalency diploma. She took the entire GED test, including mathematical calculations, graphs, and an essay, in her head, and received a special recognition award for scoring an exceptionally high 3280. She was a student speaker at the GED graduation ceremony, and received a standing ovation for her speech.

Shirley became an author at age twenty, completing three books within one year. She wrote her books using a screen reader on her computer, typing with her two index fingers at the speed of about sixty words per minute. She successfully completed every self-publishing task, including formatting her manuscripts, on her own.

In January 2006, Shirley tied for first place in Be the Star You Are! Second Annual Essay Contest founded by New York Times bestselling author, TV/radio personality Cynthia Brian, garnering her a third appearance on Cynthia's live radio show. Shirley's winning entry, titled *The Jewel from Heavenly Father*, is dedicated to her beloved mother Juliet Cheng. In the following January,

Shirley won Honorable Mention in the same contest for her essay, *I Hold the Power*, her personal story of overcoming blindness at the age of seventeen. In January 2008, Shirley was yet again one of the winners in the contest, earning Honorable Mention for her essay, *My Mother: A Fighter, a Victor, a Lover*, which applauds her stellar mother for being a courageous and loving fighter to protect her life at all costs.

Shirley has an immense passion for life and is full of life and vigor. Despite her severe disabilities, Shirley has striven to overcome overwhelming obstacles and she is living the life she loves, while she empowers, inspires, and motivates others to do the same.

Shirley has extraordinary goals with the aspiration of attending college at Harvard University, where she plans to earn doctorates in microbiology, zoology, astronomy, physiology, and pathology, after a successful eye surgery.

Shirley is a true magical gift, a star with endless shine.

Shirley As an Advocate

Besides advocating parental rights in children's medical care, Shirley is also an advocate of aide/caregiver monitoring and screening for students with special needs and disabled people.

She was mistreated and abused by one-on-one aides when she attended school. "The trouble with uncaring aides actually lies with the authorities," she says. "If they had listened to my complaints and kept a close watch on the aides, I wouldn't have gone through all the suffering."

Other Books by Shirley Cheng

• Waking Spirit: Prose & Poems the Spirit Sings (with foreword by New York Times bestselling author Cynthia Brian)
ISBN: 978-0-6151-3680-6 (trade paperback)
978-0-6151-3893-0 (hardback)
• *Embrace Ultra-Ability! Wisdom, Insight & Motivation from the Blind Who Sees Far and Wide*
ISBN: 978-0-6151-5522-7
• *Daring Quests of Mystics*
ISBN: 978-1-4116-5664-2
• *The Revelation of a Star's Endless Shine: A Young Woman's Autobiography of 20-Year Victories over Victimization*
(with foreword by Cynthia Brian)
ISBN: 978-0-6151-5044-4
• *Dance with Your Heart: Tales and Poems That the Heart Tells*
ISBN: 978-1-4116-1858-9
• *The Adventures of a Blind and Physically Disabled Award-Winning Author: Inspiration & Motivation to Empower You to Go for Your Own Gold Medals*
ISBN: 978-0-6151-7515-7

With highly acclaimed experts, including Dr. Wayne Dyer, Tony Robbins, Jack Canfield, and John Gray, Shirley co-authored *Wake Up...Live the Life You Love: Finding Life's Passion* in the bestselling *Wake Up...Live the Life You Love* series and *101 Great Ways to Improve Your Life, Volume 2.*

Book Awards

Waking Spirit: Prose & Poems the Spirit Sings is the recipient of:

- Mom's Choice Awards in Inspirational/Motivational
- The Avatar Award for Spiritual Excellence in Literature (2008)
- Best book in three categories of Reader Views 2007 Annual Literary Awards: First Place in Poetry Nonfiction, and Second Place in both New Age Nonfiction and Spirituality/Inspiration
- Finalist in the national Indie Excellence 2007 Book Awards
- Honorable Mention in the 2007 New York Book Festival Competition in Poetry
- Honorable Mention in the 2007 DIY Book Festival in Poetry

Embrace Ultra-Ability! Wisdom, Insight & Motivation from the Blind Who Sees Far and Wide is the recipient of:

- Reader Views 2008 Literary Awards – Honorable Mention for Body/Mind/Spirit
- Nine Parent to Parent Adding Wisdom Awards
- Finalist in the 2008 Next Generation Indie Book Awards in Motivational
- Finalist in the National Best Books 2008 Awards in Philosophy

Shirley on the WWW

Visit Shirley on the Web at http://www.shirleycheng.com to learn more about her, her books, listen to some of her radio show interviews, e-mail her, and subscribe to her monthly newsletter, *Inspiration from a Blind*, to receive words of inspiration, special news and events information, and exclusive offers for members. Her newsletter issues are archived on her blog, http://blog.shirleycheng.com to which people can subscribe via e-mail or RSS.

Personalized autographed copies of all of Shirley's books are available from her website.

Her books are also available through Ingram, from Amazon.com (and their international sites) and BN.com, and also available through brick-and-mortar Waldenbooks and Borders stores.

Shirley is available for interviews, speaking engagements, book signings, and inspirational events.

www.ingramcontent.com/pod-product-compliance
Lightning Source LLC
Chambersburg PA
CBHW030017290326
41934CB00005B/376